David L. Laing

Thinking and Drinking
A Cocktail Party of the Minds

Cosmic Art Center

Cosmic Art Center
62 Cedar St.
Apt. 601
Seattle, Washington 98121

Paperback ISBN: 978-1-960089-08-3

Dedicated to Those Who Achieve
Inebriation from Imagination

Foreword

From the imagination of visionary (and somewhat eccentric) writer and artist David L. Laing comes **Thinking and Drinking: A Cocktail Party of the Minds**.

T.S. Eliot and Erik Satie cordially invite you to a cocktail party with some of the greatest minds in history. Erik politely demands that guests dress in all white. Notable guests include Socrates, Shakespeare, Benjamin Franklin, Einstein, Beethoven, Charles Dickens, Ernest Hemingway, Thomas Edison, Nikola Tesla, Van Gogh, Sigmund Freud, Nietzsche, Mary Shelley, Oscar Wilde, George Sand, Edgar Allan Poe, Nostradamus, Groucho Marx, a 30,000-year-old cave man, and a polar bear. Hemingway will likely need a ride home.

What would happen if history's greatest thinkers, philosophers, scientists, artists, musicians, writers, and eccentrics came together for a cocktail party, beyond the confines of time and space, in varying degrees of intoxication? Author Laing's answer is **Thinking and Drinking**, an illuminating, entertaining and delightfully bizarre thought experiment from the depths of his wild imagination.

Written in the form of a *Platonic Dialog* between these notable figures and many, many others, the magical realism and open bar in **Thinking and Drinking** allow each character to embody their most essential nature and engage with other luminaries from different eras and corners of the world that would be otherwise impossible. The dialog and interactions that unfold give insight into each person's life, as they explore their thoughts and theories, share their histories and notable quotations, and demonstrate their various neuroses.

Plato preferred to write in a dialogical form because he believed that oral communication is superior to written text. He believed that writing in the form of dialogues was useful in transmitting principles to people with the aim of spreading the concepts of his doctrine in the most congenial way.

A dialogue is a tool that mimics the way the soul tries to talk to itself. The dialogues don't stop with the book—you need to discuss it with other people afterwards. The book is a kind of flame to ignite and have it leap to another soul!

Laing invites the reader to suspend disbelief, embrace the impossible, and let your imagination and curiosity guide you through this one-of-a-kind journey.

Thinking and Drinking

The day begins to dawn over T.S. Eliot's historic London mansion. Gentle rays of early sunlight twinkle through the fog into a wide-open bedroom window, illuminating a completely nude Ben Franklin as he performs his religiously habitual morning yawn.

The bedroom door creaks open him, as T.S. Eliot enters the room and takes in the view of Franklin's bare backside.

T.S. ELIOT: I just poked my head in here to see what you were up to.

BEN FRANKLIN: I will be standing here for another half an hour taking my "air bath."

T.S. ELIOT: That explains your nude presence, to embody your morning's essence.

Franklin turns around and looks at Eliot inquisitively.

BEN FRANKLIN: ...and what's with the lipstick and green-tinted face powder?

T.S. ELIOT: My cocktail party, my house, and my show--hearty and arty!

BEN FRANKLIN: Indeed T.S.!

Eliot quickly returns to the main hall, where Fredrich Von Schiller is sitting and fervently breathing in a scent in the air.

FREDRICH VON SCHILLER: Suddenly I am possessed with inspiration to write! That scent of rotten apples is simply heaven-sent!

(He fingers dried rotten apple pieces hidden away in his pocket.)

Edgar Allan Poe appears in a white cape-like coat. Erik Satie, Eliot's co-host for the party, had already established that the dress code for the party would be all white. Poe now holds a scroll high up in his right hand.

EDGAR ALLAN POE: Where has my editor run off to. What was her name?...Sarah?!

The scroll catches Schiller's attention.

FREDRICH VON SCHILLER: How have you attached all those continuous strips of paper together?

EDGAR ALLAN POE: I have used a kind of sealing wax to fix one sheet to another. It's simply driving my editors crazy.

A white cat suddenly darts across the drawing room.

T.S. ELIOT: Whose white tabby cat?

EDGAR ALLAN POE: That's my beloved Catterina, my "literary guardian." In fact, she plays a huge role in my creative process.

FREDRICH VON SCHILLER: Please, go on!

EDGAR ALLAN POE: She will leap up on the piano and walk up and down the keys until I "hear" something.

Benjamin Franklin, now fully dressed, joins the party.

2

BEN FRANKLIN: Can I be "frank" here?

EDGAR ALLAN POE: *(Laughs)* Aren't you always.

Franklin smiles and clears his throat.

BEN FRANKLIN: Though morbid and at times gory, I am able to wade through these murky waters to follow your story.

EDGAR ALLAN POE: Why am I not surprised! By the way, glad to see you have donned "your" all white gown.

BEN FRANKLIN: Yes, yes...It's too early, though, to hit my favorite tavern, "The Bear's Claw."

T.S. ELIOT: What would you read tonight?

Franklin, apparently not hearing this, disappears into the drawing room. There he bumps into Sigmund Freud, who is seated, smoking his cigar and poised to snort a line of cocaine.

SIGMUND FREUD: Oh, hi Ben, didn't expect anyone in here. Do you mind?

BEN FRANKLIN: Do what you need to do Sigmund. After all, you're the doctor. By the way, who did you bring?

Freud looks back and down at the white powder he is about to snort.

SIGMUND FREUD: My dream!

BEN FRANKLIN: Dream! That's how I came up with the kite.

Peals of laughter explode from the living room where more guests have been arriving. Among them is the infamous Honoré de Balzac. Presently, he is well positioned at the coffee bar area.

HONORÉ DE BALZAC: Let's see, I have stopped counting but I do believe it's my tenth.

Balzac is standing next to J.S. Bach, who is also gulping down his coffee.

JOHANN SEBASTIAN BACH: It's legal here?

HONORÉ DE BALZAC: As legal as books. All I know is that your scores are 100% caffeinated!

JOHANN SEBASTIAN BACH: Just got a hold of your "La Comedie Humaine!" I am halfway through it.

Balzac matches Bach, now, cup for cup.

HONORÉ DE BALZAC: I had to turn my life into a tragedy to find the comedy!

Bach, listening with attention, goes back to his second favorite subject, coffee.

JOHANN SEBASTIAN BACH: Coffee completely pulverized in the Turkish manner has a much richer flavor than coffee ground in a coffee mill.

HONORÉ DE BALZAC: That sounds ridiculously like something I would say. I am also a fan of your "Coffee Cantata."

4

A much smaller man is also there at the coffee bar trying to get served his coffee. Balzac is completely unaware he is blocking his way as he continues on with his conversation with Bach. It is Albert Einstein, who has managed to slip into this part of the mansion. He is crushed up against the immense Balzac.

ALBERT EINSTEIN: Give me some space!

Balzac turns around and looks down at the much smaller man standing beside him.

HONORÉ DE BALZAC: Slow down!

ALBERT EINSTEIN: There is no time!

Bach, listening intently and smiling, turns to Einstein.

JOHANN SEBASTIAN BACH: By the way, whom did you bring?

ALBERT EINSTEIN: You mean what...my violin!

HONORÉ DE BALZAC: Me?! My appetite. This coffee falls into your stomach and right away there is a general commotion. Ideas begin to move.

ALBERT EINSTEIN: Like the battalions of the Grand Army of a battlefield and...

Bach talks over him.

JOHANN SEBASTIAN BACH: ...the battle takes place. Things remembered arrive at full gallop, taking to the wind.

Without any more hesitation, Einstein takes out his violin and plunges immediately into the "battlefield" of one of Bach's partitas for solo violin. After several bars into it, tears begin to stream down his face. At the end he is now smiling and turns to Balzac

ALBERT EINSTEIN: Your hunger is a thing of wonder.

HONORÉ DE BALZAC: My social ostentation is a mere facade along with my fame for being a fascinating raconteur. The hard reality is I engage in phenomenal bouts of work lasting anywhere from 14 to 16 hours per day spent at my writing table.

ALBERT EINSTEIN: I have actually heard those stories of you dressed in your white, quasi-monastic dressing gown, with your white goose quill pen, throwing down endless cups of coffee.

HONORÉ DE BALZAC: True. As you can see, I have adhered to Satie's request to come in white rather than my favorite coat of blue.

Erik Satie, co-host for this Cocktail Party along with T. S. Eliot, makes his first appearance.

ERIK SATIE: Anyone seen T.S.? I have found one of our guests who has violated our previously agreed upon dress code.

T. S. Eliot now emerges from the drawing room where the main portion of the party is set up to take place. He is wearing a white tuxedo and tails with a white carnation in his lapel.

Satie is noticeably flustered.

T.S. ELIOT: Erik! There you are! What's the problem?

ERIK SATIE: It's Vincent!

T.S. ELIOT: Van Gogh?

ERIK SATIE: Who else. He came in a Navy-blue letter-carrying coat with brass buttons.

T.S. ELIOT: Serious? But are we really that surprised? *(He laughs politely.)*

At that very moment, Van Gogh comes stumbling around, obviously having been drinking, smoking a corn cob pipe and mumbling incoherently.

VINCENT VAN GOGH: None of you look anything like "potato eaters." Where exactly am I?

Satie looks at him with disgust.

ERIK SATIE: It is true you are the only one here displaying a strikingly different hue.

VINCENT VAN GOGH: Just trying to get those blues right for my portrait of the postman, Joseph Roulin. I decided to dress up as if I were him to feel more attuned to who he really was.

T.S. ELIOT: Weren't you aware of our specifications? This is an all-white decor and no food event.

VINCENT VAN GOGH: Titanium white or zinc white?

Satie is now beside himself with exasperation and appears to be a little out of breath. He is still glaring at Van Gogh disparagingly.

ERIK SATIE: *He turns back to Van Gogh.)* Those are names of paints--we are all here at my "Church" in roles of artistic saints.

VINCENT VAN GOGH: I guess I am just that "blue note" that brings some soul to this all-white background.

T.S. ELIOT: Let's move on here. By the way, who did you bring?

VINCENT VAN GOGH: Bring?

At that very moment Paul Gauguin bursts into the room wearing a very rustic and primitive looking all white cape and white breechcloth secured by a rope belt.

PAUL GAUGUIN: Oh, there you are Vincent! *(He starts laughing.)* You look like one of your own paintings--that postman.

ERIK SATIE: Now we are talking. Welcome to our "Hall of Worship."

Satie looks approvingly at Gauguin.

PAUL GAUGUIN: I arrived in the white business suit I wore on my short trip back to Copenhagen but made a quick change here into something more comfortable. Now I am fully convinced that somehow Shakespeare just got it right!

ERIK SATIE: How so Paul?

PAUL GAUGUIN: Something definitely IS rotten in Denmark!

VINCENT VAN GOGH: Have you seen my straw chair, Gauguin. Suddenly I would just love to sit down on it and smoke my corncob pipe.

Not surprisingly, Van Gogh is clearly and completely locked away in his own private world. Behind them, out of a huge cloud of smoke, George Sand appears in her white tuxedo, very similar to the one Eliot is wearing, and also sporting a white top hat. She abandons the cigar in favor of a cigarette held in a long cigarette holder.

GEORGE SAND: Sorry I am late. Frederic had another serious coughing bout.

ERIK SATIE: Then you couldn't bring him?

GEORGE SAND: I brought my attitude to fill in for his far superior "etude."

T.S. ELIOT: We are all going to the drawing room. There is a piano there for Erik to entertain us.

ERIK SATIE: I will only play if there is no one there. If there is, hopefully they are not listening. My music is for the "background." If you got my "back," then I can cover some "ground." I play what I feel as if I were bored with the whole ordeal.

T.S. ELIOT: No worries, Erik. We have a backup.

ERIK SATIE: You mean...

T.S. ELIOT: Yes! Mr. Franz Liszt in person! A real crowd-pleaser with a crazy and faithful following. What an icebreaker for the "drawing room!"

George Sand blows a huge cloud of white smoke and heads for the drawing room too. In her wake strides Groucho Marx with his not so white cloud of smoke puffed out of his cigar. Satie immediately recognizes Groucho from his films, big hits in France, and of course because he had been invited.

ERIK SATIE: Glad to see you adhered to the dress code.

GROUCHO MARX: Huh? Code? Dress? Should I have come in a dress?

ERIK SATIE: White!

GROUCHO MARX: Yes. It is because I just saw a ghost and turned white.

ERIK SATIE: Ghost?!

GROUCHO MARX: Of myself, I brought.

ERIK SATIE: Oh, your guest?

GROUCHO MARX: No, my guest is Harpo!

ERIK SATIE: A harp?

GROUCHO MARX: Well, no, but he plays a harp.

Eliot has been listening in on the conversation with obvious enjoyment.

10

T.S. ELIOT: Hmmm...now, it seems, we have a backup for the backup.

GROUCHO MARX: What's going on here? I debated with myself whether to come or not to a party where I was invited.

Harpo is definitely there and fully present with his white "toy horn" and extra-long white "doctor's" coat. Seeing George Sand, he honks his horn and starts to follow her into the drawing room. He stands next to her too closely and stares at her face unblinkingly. Satie, upon hearing Harpo beep his horn, smiles.

ERIK SATIE: There is our true background sound. You really don't need ME!

Ben Franklin, on his own, has already provided another valuable background sound with his "Glass Armonica," of his own invention.

BEN FRANKLIN: Of all my many inventions, playing the "Glass Armonica" gives me the most satisfaction. I even painted it white in Satie's honor.

Satie hears Franklin and smiles, now pleased at the way things seem to be unfolding.

ERIK SATIE: It is what my "church" wanted. This "church" can be anywhere real people are doing what they want and love most.

Harpo honks his horn with satisfaction and in obvious agreement. Another guest arrives. It is Emilie du Chatelet, in a glamorous low-cut dress and glimmering white shawl looking mathematically well-equated.

EMILIE DU CHATELET: Erik! I have your Gymnopedie No. 1 swimming through my head. It is so grounding for my busy scientific brain.

In the meantime, Voltaire has made his way into Eliot's house. He is impatient, thinking that there may be no coffee.

VOLTAIRE: I had heard we were going to have a "coffee bar" here.

Eliot sees the two together.

T.S. ELIOT: Had no idea that you and ...

VOLTAIRE: Emilie! Yes, she is desperately attempting to teach me math; it is clearly not part of my overall path.

Emilie du Chatelet smiles at Harpo's intense flirting. Harpo grabs her and she surprisingly does not resist. He promptly lets her go, equally shocked at her lack of protest. Harpo makes sign language pantomime that he wants to take her to bed and then pretends to play his harp.

EMILIE DU CHATELET: At least, I can do all the talking with this one. I just love your white bleached hair. Is it real or a wig?

Harpo tries to yank off his hair but without any success. On the other side of the drawing room Sigmund Freud rises, obviously high on cocaine.

SIGMUND FREUD: All of you have either been a patient of mine, are presently, or soon will be.

Groucho Marx strides quickly back and forth as if deep in thought.

GROUCHO MARX: *(Talking to no one in particular.)* You calling me crazy or just not smart enough to be lazy?

Van Gogh returns in delirium holding a bloodied letter and his head bandaged, while still in his postman's clothes that had violated Satie's white dress code. He quickly goes over to Gauguin.

VINCENT VAN GOGH: Paul, hurry, take this to her! Maybe now she will listen!

PAUL GAUGUIN: What have you done!

He grabs the letter and leaves quickly. Meanwhile, Satie is completely unmoved by all this drama.

ERIK SATIE: All of us make sacrifices when we join the "Church." An eye for an eye...or in this case, an ear for an ear.

Werner Herzog arrives at the mansion wearing his only suit which he has dyed white for the occasion, and his one pair of shoes he has polished white.

T.S. ELIOT: You look bedraggled Mr. Herzog.

WERNER HERZOG: I just walked here all the way from Paris. I am in need of a new pair of shoes. I brought my camera. Is that OK?

ERIK SATIE: Yes, everyone was told to bring someone, or in your case, something.

WERNER HERZOG: I stole this 35-millimeter camera from the Munich Institute for Film Research and used it on several films, including the one we are doing tonight.

T.S. ELIOT: Excuse me, Werner. I just saw Charles Dickens come up to the house.

Charles Dickens arrives dressed in a heavy white London style greatcoat. He looks around nervously, then takes out his comb to make sure his hair is still all in place.

CHARLES DICKENS: Who arranged the furniture here?

T.S. ELIOT: I did! It's my home.

CHARLES DICKENS: Hmmm. Interesting.

He takes out his comb again to go over his hair one more time.

CHARLES DICKENS: No one is useless in this world who lightens the burdens of another.

ERIK SATIE: We all should live in free-flowing harmony based on nature and emotion!

Dickens looks down at a white hammer Satie is holding.

CHARLES DICKENS: What is that for, Erik?

ERIK SATIE: Obviously for protection!

14

CHARLES DICKENS: *(Laughs)* And you are known for simplicity and Zen-like patience.

ERIK SATIE: True, that is my science.

Dickens takes a long drink from a small vial of absinthe.

ERIK SATIE: I have been asked to perform this evening by Mr. Eliot and have politely refused.

Dickens looks around again at the furniture obviously with some special concern for how it is arranged.

ERIK SATIE: What do you think? Can you hear it?

CHARLES DICKENS: Hear what?

ERIK SATIE: The "Furniture Music."

CHARLES DICKENS: What the dickens! *(He smiles.)*

ERIK SATIE: You will--later on.

Satie walks away wearing a white cap, white stockings and a white waistcoat. Dickens calls after him.

CHARLES DICKENS: Where is your white umbrella? I have heard you own a hundred of them.

Satie is still walking away he responds.

ERIK SATIE: Why don't you "comb" the house to see if you can find one?

Dickens takes him up on it and begins to wander the house. He soon finds the bedroom and checks it to make sure that the bed is aligned North to South by using his compass. Then, taking out his pocket watch, he notices Emilie du Chatelet seated in the far corner. He goes up to her with no introduction and begins to slowly swing the watch in front of her.

CHARLES DICKENS: Keep your eye on the watch and slowly...slowly... you are becoming very drowsy.

EMILIE DU CHATELET: Hey, Mr. Dickens! Just what are you up to? What...are...you...up...to?

She falls immediately into a hypnotic trance as Dickens gets up to begin to orchestrate her movement.

CHARLES DICKENS: Go over to the only person here wearing a blue coat and tell him you are back and are ready to lend him an ear.

Emilie du Chatelet gets up and starts walking in the direction of the still agitated Van Gogh, whom she finds of course still wearing the postman's uniform. In the meantime, Lewis Carroll has arrived. His quest is for, yet another "Lewis Carroll." There are two. It appears he has found him.

LEWIS CARROLL: I am Lewis Carroll, and this is Charles Dodgson. We are two, yet we are one.

Freud returns at this exact moment in time to observe all that is happening. Satie is also taking it all in but shows no signs of perplexity or confusion.

ERIK SATIE: Both of you are of course welcome here. You can come together now or each on his own.

SIGMUND FREUD: Though I have never treated you, I believe I can help you.

LEWIS CARROLL: To whom are you referring: Mr. Dodgson?

SIGMUND FREUD: We should talk about this. I could be of help.

LEWIS CARROLL: What or to whom are you proposing to help?

SIGMUND FREUD: *(Feeling cocaine empowered)* I can cure you of being lost in your own kind of wonderland.

LEWIS CARROLL: Lost?! Have YOU lost your mind? We are both fine!

Carrol gestures to the invisible "Charles Dodgson," whom he had brought as his guest. Emilie bumps into Freud as she is still making her trance-like way to find Van Gogh to deliver the letter. Freud gazes after her.

SIGMUND FREUD: She looks to be in a deep trance. This technique of Mesmer's is in fact quite unique.

LEWIS CARROLL: Go on. I think I see a "rabbit hole" on the horizon.

SIGMUND FREUD: We are not masters of our own minds!

LEWIS CARROLL: You're telling me! Do you think I just dream of this castle-in-the-sky, or do I actually live in it?

SIGMUND FREUD: Well, if you do live in it, I can help but I'll be collecting the rent.

LEWIS CARROLL: *(Laughs)* I admit I am not well and do suffer from some brand of schizophrenia, which, until now have been able to withstand.

SIGMUND FREUD: Go on...

LEWIS CARROLL: What I deeply fear is that if you "cure" me I'll never write again.

SIGMUND FREUD: Interesting.

In the background we continue to hear Franklin playing his "Glass Armonica." Emilie du Chatelet, still hypnotized, finally encounters Van Gogh. Van Gogh looks up somewhat startled.

VINCENT VAN GOGH: You look familiar.

Emilie looks back at him in a blank stare and then speaks in a monotone.

EMILIE DU CHATELET: I have come to lend you an ear.

Van Gogh becomes giddy with excitement.

VINCENT VAN GOGH: As you can see, I am in need of one!

Dickens, who has been observing the two, now approaches them. Van Gogh looks up at him.

VINCENT VAN GOGH: Aren't you that English...

CHARLES DICKENS: Yes! I am cursed to have a name that is a curse word, created by none other than Shakespeare.

VINCENT VAN GOGH: Did you have anything to do with her coming over to me?

CHARLES DICKENS: Yes, I have always been interested in the paranormal. As a matter of fact, I am part of an investigating group here in London called: "The Ghost Club."

Van Gogh looks at Emilie then back at Dickens, adjusts his blue mailman's coat and lightly touches his bandaged ear.

VINCENT VAN GOGH: I...I...do need some help.

EMILIE DU CHATELET: *(Speaking in monotone)* That--is-- why--I--am--here.

Dickens snaps his fingers, and she abruptly comes out of it. She looks slightly confused and a bit dazed, then suddenly recognizes Van Gogh from his self-portraits.

EMILIE DU CHATELET: Vincent?!

VINCENT VAN GOGH: I am not that postman I have painted, but his alter ego, here to bring a message of emotion and color none of us should forego.

Emilie then points to the window looking out from the mansion.

EMILIE DU CHATELET: There is your "Starry Night!" Let's go bathe in it!

At this moment Ken Kesey barges into Eliot's mansion accompanied by the Big Chief Bromden carrying his broom. He had just parked his "Merry Prankster" bus, "Further," outside the mansion.

KEN KESEY: *(Bursting out)* To hell with facts! We need stories!

Eliot, as well as the rest, are a bit taken back by the intrusion.

T.S. ELIOT: How about the one we are creating here in my drawing room cocktail party?

KEN KESEY: Cocktail party? Who needs drinks? Bring on the psychedelics!

T.S. ELIOT: Psycho...what?

KEN KESEY: Oh, forget it! I've got a stash in "Further."

T.S. ELIOT: Further?

KEN KESEY: My bus!

T.S. ELIOT: You took the bus here?

KEN KESEY: Now I do need a drink, and fast!

George Bernard Shaw is now making his entry as well. He has donned a white shawl to protect himself from the cold and appears to be distracted by something.

GEORGE BERNARD SHAW: How can I write here? This room does not turn. It should be revolving.

T.S. ELIOT: Wow! I thought I was eccentric. Maybe he's already got what this Kesey character is after.

20

GEORGE BERNARD SHAW: Yes, mounted on a revolving mechanism, so that as I work, I can follow the sun throughout the day.

Satie is listening in and responds to Shaw's request.

ERIK SATIE: Mr. Shaw, you are here for the party, a cocktail party-- not to work. By the way, nice white shawl.

GEORGE BERNARD SHAW: Is that you Erik? You have come here to the foreground. Is that why I don't hear your piano sound?

ERIK SATIE: You mean my furniture music...that comes a little later.

Freud is now gazing around the room at the guests.

SIGMUND FREUD: Wow! There is a lot of work to be done here. I came to the right spot.

Heraclitus, himself, now ambles into the main hallway. His white toga is in shambles, full of dust from the road and torn in places from the brambles.

ERIK SATIE: Heraclitus it is, right?! Your reputation precedes you. It looks as though you have tried stepping into that river more than once. *(He laughs.)*

We hear a sudden crash of lightning then the thunder roar.

HERACLITUS: Thunderbolt steers all things.

T.S. ELIOT: *(Smiling)* You brought this change in weather?

HERACLITUS: It brought me as well as us all.

At that very moment the ceiling overhead opens up and someone begins to descend from a basket. T. S. Eliot looks up, slightly smiling, in quiet anticipation of what he, himself, had previously set up. This was to be one of the main attractions of the Cocktail Party. None other than Socrates is now being lowered in the basket.

T.S. ELIOT: Welcome to London, Socrates. I imagine way up there is better to observe the sun and other meteorological phenomena.

Socrates climbs out of the basket wearing a clean white toga.

SOCRATES: What kind of "thinkery" have we here?

ERIK SATIE: It is our new "Church," which is why we are all in white...well, almost all.

Satie's eyes roam the room to eventually come to rest on Van Gogh in his blue postman's uniform, contentedly speaking to Emilie du Chatelet.

Eliot quickly adds his comment.

T.S. ELIOT: It's...eh...my cocktail party officially or...unofficially.

He glances over at Satie nearby.

T.S. ELIOT: A kind of church party.

SOCRATES: As anyone can see, I am in good physical shape, except for my face. *(He tries to hide it.)* It keeps betraying me of my public and personal space. I can't mock it but others sure can.

Socrates is looking around as if trying to spot someone he believes should be there.

T.S. ELIOT: Can I show you around?

SOCRATES: I don't see him anywhere.

T.S. ELIOT: Who?

SOCRATES: Aristophanes!

T.S. ELIOT: Not sure if I even invited him.

SOCRATES: He has suddenly become my own worst nightmare after he wrote and performed "the Clouds."

Satie now comes back into the room where everyone has congregated overhearing Socrates.

ERIK SATIE: Aristophanes. He was a last-minute addition but I never got a confirmation.

Socrates attempts to mask his face at that moment as Eliot tries to change the subject.

T.S. ELIOT: Did you bring a guest?

SOCRATES: Yes!...My lack of knowledge! I am excited to share "nothing" with anybody and everybody.

ERIK SATIE: Wow! *(Quietly)* I love this guy.

SOCRATES: Speaking of masks, yours is intriguing.

T.S. ELIOT: Oh, you mean the lipstick or the green-tinted face powder?

SOCRATES: Either. Why didn't I ever think of that?

ERIK SATIE: Because you know nothing?

There is another clap of thunder from the raging storm brought by Heraclitus. A carriage now pulls up behind Kesey's bus "Further," as wind and rain continue on. A bedraggled, short, stocky man with wild hair emerges and heads for the mansion door. On cue, Franklin plays the opening to the Fifth at the exact moment there is a knock at the door. Another time by Franklin and another knock. As Eliot opens the door a strong gust of wind enters the mansion.

T.S. ELIOT: It's Beethoven!

LUDWIG VAN BEETHOVEN: Who?! Whoever it is, I am here! Whatever I can't hear, I CAN write!

Freud is still looking on, observing everything.

SIGMUND FREUD: This is one "patient" I think I'll pass on.

Beethoven heads to the drawing room unaccompanied. Eliot turns in Satie's direction and stares at his hair.

T.S. ELIOT: By the way Erik, why are you going gray?

ERIK SATIE: It just looks gray but it's really white.

Already in the drawing room Beethoven does not hesitate to create a commotion and starts to yell.

LUDWIG VAN BEETHOVEN: I need a bucket of cold water! Now! Somebody get it!

Satie leaves to get it and then quickly returns as Beethoven grabs it and empties it over his head onto the drawing room rug.

LUDWIG VAN BEETHOVEN: Inspiration! I got it!

Beethoven then starts searching through all his pockets for something to write on and a quill pen, which he finds immediately and starts to vigorously write down his ideas. The attention now shifts to Charles Dickens as he reappears with a new idea and turns directly to Satie.

CHARLES DICKENS: Let's have a white Christmas tonight!

ERIK SATIE: I am one step ahead of you. I already ordered a white tree.

Van Gogh and Emilie du Chatelet are still conversing with enthusiasm as Van Gogh offers her an absinthe.

EMILIE DU CHATELET: What is it?

VINCENT VAN GOGH: Absinthe!

Franklin has stopped playing his "glass armonica" and is at the bar.

BEN FRANKLIN: Madeira! Please!

Franklin gestures toward Joe, the resident bartender.

JOE: What does this oxidized, fortified wine do for you?

BEN FRANKLIN: *(Laughing)* Gets me as high as a kite.

Joe pauses, then gets it and laughs too. Without anyone noticing, F. Scott Fitzgerald has arrived on the scene and to no one's surprise is already at the bar.

F. SCOTT FITZGERALD: Gin rickey, sir.

JOE: Can I just come out and say it?

F. SCOTT FITZGERALD: Go ahead. You won't be the first.

JOE: First you take a drink, then the drink...

F. SCOTT FITZGERALD: ...takes a drink, then...

JOE: ...the drink takes you!

F. SCOTT FITZGERALD: I love gin because it isn't easy to detect on your breath.

Suddenly the mansion lights flicker then go off and come right back on again due to the wildness of the storm. At that moment Thomas Edison arrives.

T.S. ELIOT: My namesake, Thomas, what an unexpected pleasure. I know you have been completely immersed in your own work for quite some time.

THOMAS EDISON: Too many assumptions, T.S. I have eschewed such necessities as sleeping by adopting a polyphasic sleep cycle, my nap- oriented sleep pattern aims to free up more waking time over a person's life.

T.S. ELIOT: You are "lights out" one of our most inventive minds.

THOMAS EDISON: *(Smiling)* I have been called illuminated!

T.S. ELIOT: How many geniuses does it take...

THOMAS EDISON: To change a light bulb?

Before Eliot can respond George Bernard Shaw reappears obviously reinvigorated and has just overheard the joke setup.

GEORGE BERNARD SHAW: Two! One to hold the bulb and one to turn my "revolving shack mechanism."

Edison looks confused at the intrusion and his bizarre conclusion.

THOMAS EDISON: Have we met?

GEORGE BERNARD SHAW: Probably not. I'm usually outside. The best place to find God is in a garden. You can dig for him there.

Ernest Hemingway has now made his entrance wearing his white Cuban style suit and white fedora smoking a Cuban cigar.

ERNEST HEMINGWAY: Where can I find Eliot?

Satie shows up to help out.

ERIK SATIE: Right this way Mr. Hemingway.

ERNEST HEMINGWAY: Are you that "white fish" guy who plays piano at the "Chat Noir?"

ERIK SATIE: Yes, a man of contrasts: white fish, black cat, white keys, black keys.

Eliot now arrives to meet Hemingway.

T.S. ELIOT: Heard you were in Spain, then Africa, then Cuba...

ERNEST HEMINGWAY: And now London.

He pauses a split second then blurts out loudly.

ERNEST HEMINGWAY: Thomas! I just got to tell someone! I can't write anymore. I am finished!

T.S. ELIOT: Maybe Freud can help. He is here. Are you familiar with his work?

ERNEST HEMINGWAY: I have creative paralysis--does that mean that I need analysis?

Right on cue Freud enters, still high on cocaine, his senses have sharpened remarkably.

SIGMUND FREUD: Excuse me Hemingway for being blunt, but I know you are addicted to the hunt. Am I right?

Hemingway appears to have been caught off guard.

ERNEST HEMINGWAY: Hunt?...hunting...hmmmm...why...maybe, yes!

28

SIGMUND FREUD: The "hunt" has come back to haunt you. Now, YOU are no more the hunter, but the hunted.

ERNEST HEMINGWAY: What does all that mean?

SIGMUND FREUD: It is why you are now obsessed with killing yourself.

ERNEST HEMINGWAY: You definitely got my attention Dr. Freud-- what do I do now?

SIGMUND FREUD: We are all flawed. I, myself, am hooked on cocaine, which does in fact ease the pain that loves to live inside my brain.

Satie rushes over with something "important" to disclose.

ERIK SATIE: I have a little announcement. Dickens has said there will be no white Christmas. It was all a white lie.

Edison turns back to Eliot.

T.S. ELIOT: Who did you bring?

THOMAS EDISON: *(Smiling)* It's my "outlet."

Eliot looks quizzically at Edison as the lights to the mansion flicker. He then laughs a little.

T.S. ELIOT: You've connected us all here!

Outside now, the storm continues to rage on. In the middle of it all, Nikola Tesla magically appears out of nowhere. He has arrived in one of "his" cars, gets out and begins to walk around the mansion three times before even thinking about entering. Satie comes to finally let Tesla into the party.

ERIK SATIE: I can see you brought a pigeon here and white, no less. You are both very welcome.

Nikola Tesla is now aboard and approaches the two. He looks down at his white pigeon and smiles.

NIKOLA TESLA: We are all held together like stars in the firmament, with ties inseparable. These ties cannot be seen, but we can feel them.

ERIK SATIE: You came to the right place, Nikola, and you're dressed appropriately. Would you care for a glass of white wine?

NIKOLA TESLA: Wine? No, but I would love a "White Russian," the principle saving grace of their multi-cultured race! This lightning storm reminds me of my day of birth. My mother told me that she had said to the midwife I would be a "child of light."

ERIK SATIE: Fortunately, there is plenty of "white light" here.

NIKOLA TESLA: I can clearly see.

ERIK SATIE: Thomas Edison has come too.

NIKOLA TESLA: Edison! My nemesis! *(He lightly laughs.)* My former employer. I remember his absolute contempt for book learning and mathematical knowledge.

Eliot now strides over to meet and welcome Tesla.

30

T.S. ELIOT: Greetings Nikola! I imagine you are referring to Edison. Yes, he trusted himself entirely to his inventor's instinct and practical American sense.

ERIK SATIE: Your prodigious memory, Tesla, is legendary. It has been said with your photographic memory you could memorize entire books and have flashes of genius conceiving solutions to problems.

At that moment we see another flash of lightning from the raging storm and hear the thunderous response. Tesla comes inside and approaches bar to get his "White Russian," as Edison watches him intently.

NIKOLA TESLA: Hello Thomas, did you bring her?

THOMAS EDISON: Who?

NIKOLA TESLA: Your 16-year-old wife!

THOMAS EDISON: No, she was at her own "sweet sixteen" party.

NIKOLA TESLA: I ended up digging ditches after leaving you before I was able to start up my own company.

Eliot now turns to Edison to speak "directly" to him regarding his "current" status.

T.S. ELIOT: When we contacted you "directly," we were not sure you could come.

ERIK SATIE: So Tesla is our "current alternative."

NIKOLA TESLA: I am very comfortable being the "alternate" choice if I may speak "directly."

Eliot starts to laugh at their "conversational spark."

T.S. ELIOT: He can't hold a candle to you!

Fortunately, neither Edison nor Tesla hear this last comment by Eliot.

ERIK SATIE: To whom were you referring?

Eliot compulsively touches his face where his green powder is beginning to wear off and leaves a smudge. There is some more commotion outside in the storm with the arrival of another illustrious guest. Eliot goes to the door to open it.

T.S. ELIOT: Herr Nietzsche! You made it, cape and all.

FRIEDRICH NIETZSCHE: Well, you made it so clear on the white decor. I managed to grab this white cape from the theater down the road from my house at the last minute.

ERIK SATIE: How did you get here?

FRIEDRICH NIETZSCHE: Walked!

ERIK SATIE: Over 200 miles?

FRIEDRICH NIETZSCHE: The sedentary life is the very sin against the Holy Spirit. Only thoughts reached by walking have value.

ERIK SATIE: (smiling) Nice touch to dye that epic mustache of yours white!

FRIEDRICH NIETZSCHE: By the way, whose horse is that just outside in front of the mansion?

T.S. ELIOT: I have no idea.

FRIEDRICH NIETZSCHE: Please don't let anyone whip him...or her!

George Sand reappears, this time smoking a rare white "collector's cigar."

GEORGE SAND: Your mustache does not frighten me, Friedrich. There is not much I have not seen.

FRIEDRICH NIETZSCHE: One must still have chaos in oneself to be able to give birth to the dancing star.

He starts to move, dance and to remove his clothes.

ERIK SATIE: *(Bursting out suddenly)* Has anyone seen Puchillela, Mr. Scarlatti's white cat?

George Sand is thoroughly enjoying the show, especially watching Nietzsche disrobing. Einstein is back, still with his violin and playing music for this impromptu "Nietzsche Dance." Seeing Nietzsche disrobing, Satie's face turns white.

ERIK SATIE: Herr Nietzsche, please put your clothes back on!

Now at the bar, Eliot inquires if Socrates has been offered a drink.

JOE: Yes, he personally told me that the last time he accepted a drink he didn't last. Look, there he is!

SOCRATES: I do what I must, the others of talent do what they can trust. Aristophanes! Is that you! Don't tell me YOU have arrived. Suddenly I see "clouds" coming my way.

There is another strike of lightning heard coming from the continuing storm outside.

ALBERT EINSTEIN: A quiet and modest life brings more joy than a pursuit of success bound with constant unrest.

Socrates has begun to mingle and converse with his customary candor and seeming nonchalance of his glory days in the streets of Athens. He now turns to Einstein.

SOCRATES: My problem with Aristophanes is that he constantly makes me laugh, making it ever so much harder to be hostile towards him and his comedic craft.

ALBERT EINSTEIN: There are no absolute jokes. All humor is relative.

SOCRATES: I try to engage in conversation to probe the roots of my listener's belief system. Aristophanes calls what we have here at this party a "thinkery!"

ALBERT EINSTEIN: As the French love to say: "Tout comprendre c'est tout partommer" or in English: To understand everything is to forgive everything.

SOCRATES: Wasn't it our friend Buddha who first said that?

ALBERT EINSTEIN: Yes, absolutely, my relative.

Einstein picks up his violin again to follow the emotion of the storm and wind outside.

ERIK SATIE: I noticed you are without socks and the temperature is dropping.

ALBERT EINSTEIN: Yes, I was looking for white ones as you requested but didn't have any. I have reached an age when, if someone tells me to wear socks, I don't have to.

ERIK SATIE: I see.

ALBERT EINSTEIN: Are you sure it was Heraclitus who brought these storms and not Aristophanes with his "clouds" and turbulent weather forms?

SOCRATES: How did I get to be called "the gadfly of Athens?" All I ever asked for is "free maintenance by the state."

ALBERT EINSTEIN: In other words, a free handout.

SOCRATES: Not free--I'd be "teaching."

ALBERT EINSTEIN: Things like pushing the knowledge boundaries by simply posing the right questions?

SOCRATES: It is not my long white hair, bare feet or torn white cloak that charms soldiers, prostitutes, merchants and aristocrats.

ALBERT EINSTEIN: You have been called the true father of western thought.

SOCRATES: Even with my disturbingly ugly face, a potbelly, a weird walk, swiveling eyes and hairy hands?

ALBERT EINSTEIN: It was your simple pronouncement of all the "things" you do not need that eventually let you formulate your "know nothing" creed.

Satie approaches the two icons.

ERIK SATIE: You seemed to have enjoyed a peculiar kind of private piety while the rest of Athens at that time was focused on a religious public display of exuberance as its center performance.

At that moment the spirit of Aristophanes appears in a "cloud" right there in the main hallway of Eliot's mansion. From inside the cloud Aristophanes begins to speak.

ARISTOPHANES: You, Socrates, fear the emerging power of the written word will diminish the face-to-face contact of your own "teaching room"--the "agora."

SOCRATES: To merely catalog the world and not lead it will cause its ultimate downfall.

ARISTOPHANES: You mean it won't happen from a rain cloud's thunderbolt?

SOCRATES: That would be a mere jolt.

ARISTOPHANES: Why do you need my "rain" when you already have the purest water in midday as the sun heats the brain.

They say because your ideas are refreshing and nourishing you have been given the nickname, "source."

SOCRATES: Not the "source" but the "mouth," no brainiac grey-beard but just a bustling, energetic, wine-swilling, sword-bearing veteran who is here to be heard, not to hide behind the hatred of the herd.

ARISTOPHANES: I am here to cloud your imagination and poke fun at your influence upon our nation.

SOCRATES: Life is full of questions. Idiots are full of answers.

In the background we hear the sound of a wild harpsichord being played. It is none other than Domenico Scarlatti. Suddenly a white cat leaps up onto his harpsichord and walks back and forth on the keys.

DOMENICO SCARLATTI: Puchillela! Where have you been?

Satie also appears calling for Puchillela as if it were his own cat.

ERIK SATIE: What are you doing on that harpsichord?

DOMENICO SCARLATTI: Let her "play!" That's what cats do!

ERIK SATIE: She is obviously yours by the way you connect?

DOMENICO SCARLATTI: Of course!

ERIK SATIE: Please excuse me. I took her in as mine since she is all white.

Puchillela continues playing then suddenly leaps off to the floor and looks up at Scarlatti.

DOMENICO SCARLATTI: She began playing on a "wrong note" that she instinctively made "right." I should follow in her "sound tracks."

Scarlatti then finishes what Puchillela started and calls it the "Cat Sonata."

ERIK SATIE: Impressive Domenico! Your striking harmonies, sudden contrasts of texture and bold dissonances remind me of improvised forms of dances.

DOMENICO SCARLATTI: "Puchillela" taught me the virtues of beginning on a "wrong note" or chord then trying to fix it into contrasting concord.

ERIK SATIE: Individuality is the central feature of each compositional picture.

Beethoven now begins to "feel" the music of Scarlatti through the floorboards of Eliot's drawing room as he yells out.

LUDWIG VAN BEETHOVEN: You possess one of the most original creative minds I have ever "seen," since I can't hear what you are doing.

Satie, in the middle of all this ruckus, turns to Scarlatti to comment on his attire.

ERIK SATIE: Thank you so much for making your wardrobe sacrifice. I know for a fact that being of a quiet and grave nature you always dressed in black.

Beethoven yells out again now even more excited and agitated.

LUDWIG VAN BEETHOVEN: You play that harpsichord like ten hundred devils!

ERIK SATIE: You are confident, not just carefree, and at times recklessly capricious.

DOMENICO SCARLATTI: I am as surprised as you embarking in directions that even I could not anticipate.

ERIK SATIE: It has been called ingenious jesting with art, a kind of sound jousting straight from the start.

LUDWIG VAN BEETHOVEN: Your highly inventive keyboard stroke takes you far beyond the conventional palette of Baroque.

DOMENICO SCARLATTI: For so long I have been used to devising musical evenings in Philip V's court. I had to cheer him up from his manic depression daily.

ERIK SATIE: You express both elation and despair, which no doubt in Philip's Court cleared the air.

DOMENICO SCARLATTI: I drew from the extremes of the Iberian psyche literally everything I knew. Spinning these fascinating patterns provided that much needed distraction and content for each evening's attraction.

Einstein holds up his violin and chimes in.

ALBERT EINSTEIN: I tried many a time to play your "Cat Sonata" on my fiddle but could never solve its own spacetime riddle.

T.S. ELIOT: *(Laughing)* You of all people, Albert.

DOMENICO SCARLATTI: When I cross over my hands, I give myself away as a compulsive keyboard gambler--my fingers try and control what is deep within that wayward ambler.

Harpo dances and whirls around and then stands near the harpsichord and gestures as if playing the harp.

ERIK SATIE: Oh Harpo, it's a harpsichord, not a harp.

Harpo honks his horn and gestures playing a keyboard as Satie gets it and nods.

ERIK SATIE: Oh, yes. A harpsichord is a harp with a keyboard.

Harpo opens a closet door and goes inside and shuts the door, then comes right out and gestures playing the harp again. Scarlatti laughs heartily.

DOMENICO SCARLATTI: He is saying that a harpsichord is a harp in a box.

Harpo honks his horn loudly and smiles ridiculously wide. He sees Chatelet moving past him and turns to run after her with his white wig bouncing and long white "laboratory coat" flying. In another far corner of the drawing room sits Nostradamus

40

meditating over a brass bowl filled with water. Edgar Allen Poe has returned to the room and notices him.

EDGAR ALLAN POE: Who is that character in an obviously herbal-induced haze entering into a trance?

T.S. ELIOT: I have been told it's Nostradamus, one of Satie's invites.

The Inquisition could not force upon him a "cure" because he wrote his "quatrains" purposely cryptic and obscure.

EDGAR ALLAN POE: Didn't his fellow physicians call him an embarrassment, while the religious people thought he was possessed, and still others were convinced of his genius.

ERIK SATIE: We decided to invite him because he predicted this very event to be held here in your mansion in London!

T.S. ELIOT: I even heard right down to that very detail of Socrates arriving down through the roof in a basket as if descending from the "Clouds of Aristophanes."

EDGAR ALLAN POE: That's truly scary! I may need the "Raven" here in a hurry!

T.S. ELIOT: *(Chuckling)* Look! He is still lost in his herbal-induced haze, while possibly visualizing the creation of new worlds or cities ablaze.

EDGAR ALLAN POE: I know that early on, even before his study of medicine, his grandfather had introduced him to the ancient rites of the Jewish Tradition and the Celestial Sciences of

Astrology, giving him his first exposure to the idea of the heavens and how they drive human destiny.

Nostradamus rises as if in a trance.

NOSTRADAMUS: A man clothed in ancient robes will arrive here with art from other globes. Once again, the old will invigorate the new--drops of knowledge appearing like morning dew.

EDGAR ALLAN POE: We are witnessing a new quatrain spoken in his classically rhymed four-line verses, where an ancient artist comes to introduce all of us to new universes.

Poe's cat "Catterina" is now playing with Scarlatti's cat "Puchillela," two white balls of snow tumbling together in a cleverly orchestrated side-show.

T.S. ELIOT: You are beginning to make a refrain like Nostradamus speaking in a quatrain.

EDGAR ALLAN POE: When I get my chance to "dance" I can "see" without entering into an herbal trance.

T.S. ELIOT: I guess we will see if Nostradamus is right about that visionary in ancient robes bringing us his latest inspirational probes.

Nostradamus, still in a trance, starts to glide around the drawing room. Charles Dickens notices Nostradamus wandering around in a kind of daze and also sees Poe walking away mumbling something.

EDGAR ALLAN POE: Presents an infinitude of pulsating universes alternately willed into orbital systems, reactively condensed into primary particles by an infinitude of gods.

CHARLES DICKENS: What in the dickens! I am forced again to swear in my own name. *(He laughs.)* And I thought the characters I created were strange till I came here. Once again, we have reality trumping fiction.

T.S. ELIOT: Don't worry Charles, the best is yet to come.

Socrates continues his walking and "teaching" in this newly restricted area of Eliot's mansion.

T.S. ELIOT: What are you up to Socrates? Why are you staring as if looking straight through me.

SOCRATES: Though I was recognized for my valiant efforts on the battlefield, I am like any typical masculine Athenian. Just look at my stature: short and stocky with a snub nose, and as you say, bulging eyes.

Aristophanes, still invisible inside his hanging cloud, starts laughing hysterically.

ARISTOPHANES: You are harder on yourself than I ever was with you. You are your own teacher of self-mockery.

SOCRATES: It's just a way for us to clear the air here?

T.S. ELIOT: All history is stored in that "cloud" you brought.

SOCRATES: No, not the cloud, I brought only my questioning mind deep in thought.

ERIK SATIE: They say there was always a cloud hanging over you.

Trumpets sound at the mansion entrance, the bard, Shakespeare, is arriving on horseback bearing plays in his saddlebags. Aristophanes responds still concealed in his cloud.

ARISTOPHANES: Ugh! I have this kind of competition!

T.S. ELIOT: Mr. Shakespeare, we have awaited your arrival with bated breath. Now you are present in flesh and blood, a literary tower of strength. Please don't hesitate to be cruel to be kind, and above all don't just vanish into thin air.

SHAKESPEARE: I won't stay long as there is no foul play at your party during the night or throughout day.

T.S. ELIOT: We are here for comedy, not tragedy. As proof, we have Aristophanes hidden in his cloud preparing our very next spoof.

SHAKESPEARE: Good! I didn't come to work but to play, yet I am often confused as to which is which to this day.

ERIK SATIE: You too?

SHAKESPEARE: If all the year were playing holidays; to sport would be as tedious as to work.

T.S. ELIOT: From your King Henry IV, Part 1

SHAKESPEARE: All I need is one fan to continue my literary success plan!

ARISTOPHANES: *(Booming from his cloud)* Sounds like pure laziness to me. Are you sure you even wrote all those plays?

SHAKESPEARE: A blast from the distant past is only as strong as its voice will last--amply supported by the talent of a cast.

ARISTOPHANES: Any questions I refer you to Socrates, who will surely answer you with his own question.

SHAKESPEARE: It is not in the clouds or in the stars to hold our destiny but in ourselves.

ARISTOPHANES: Socrates is easy to spot as he is the one in the tattered white toga --the only one he's got.

The two white cats playing, Puchillela and Catterina roll their way over nearing the harpsichord where Scarlatti has just gotten up from the bench. First Puchillela then Catterina jump up onto the keys and start walking back and forth again. Scarlatti stops in his tracks to observe their fun and then listens.

DOMENICO SCARLATTI: It's a new "Cat Fugue." This time for four hands...or in this case, paws--clearly at work to play under their own musical laws.

Outside the storm continues raging on as Beethoven becomes more and more agitated. It now seems as though the cloud with Aristophanes inside is in sync with the storm and larger clouds outside. It is also getting colder and colder as Mid-winter is fast approaching. Now there is a new knock on the mansion door, but this time is much stronger. Eliot goes to fling open the door. A giant of a "man" stands before him clothed in white polar bear furs.

TELLENMAGNUM: Call me Tellenmagnum!

He brandishes a nine-foot-long ivory spear (white on white). Satie arrives at the door too.

ERIK SATIE: polar bear white! Fantastic!

As Tellenmagnum holds up his ivory spear we can see that at its opposite end is an equally large paint brush.

TELLENMAGNUM: If it had been snowing, I would have come in my sled pulled by eight giant white huskies.

Eliot turns to Satie with a sudden inspiring thought:

T.S. ELIOT: Could this be that man "clothed in ancient robes" that Nostradamus saw in his brass bowl filled with water?

Tellenmagnum can't help but overhear.

TELLENMAGNUM: Not could, but am--that same hunter/artist who turned cave walls into highly imaginative painted halls.

Nostradamus reappears out of his trance, fully aware and conscious.

NOSTRADAMUS: What did I say that would come in ancient robes by day and bring us new light by night?

A strange and eerie hum now emanates from Tellenmagnum.

TELLENMAGNUM: Do you hear the sound of my "aura?" It is strongest at dawn, as we called our aurora, our acoustic "agora." It is the sound meeting place where we sing and paint our own hallowed space. An inner light then illuminated the "cave of our night."

Van Gogh struggles into the main hall, still in a kind of a daze from his recent encounter with Emile du Chatelet, to witness all the commotion of Tellenmagnum's arrival. The bandage around his ear is gone.

VINCENT VAN GOGH: Art that you can hear would give us a new start, from that first cave to inside a cathedral nave!

TELLENMAGNUM: You are an artist! If you paint, you come with the blessing of a saint.

VINCENT VAN GOGH: I am no saint but a sinner who just happens to paint.

Satie kept staring at those polar bear furs and now reaches over to touch and feel their white softness.

TELLENMAGNUM: When I got your "invitation" I was awakened from 30,000 years of hibernation!

NOSTRADAMUS: I saw your image in my brass bowl and now you are miraculously here for our drawing room show.

T.S. ELIOT: I call this art and music a kind of mellow madness, an excellent antidote for any seasonal sadness.

TELLENMAGNUM: Acoustics were even more important than what we painted on the walls. It was in that inner chamber that chamber music first began. Its sound was scored on the stone making its mark of the tone.

ERIK SATIE: I love that! The tone of the stone! It's not just white noise but sound played with poise.

Socrates is still wearing his light tattered toga, walking with his distinctive gait, barefoot as always and heading toward the door where Eliot has decided to wait.

SOCRATES: I feel I am being made fun of by friends at a Great Party.

TELLENMAGNUM: I will be no party to that. You appear to be someone of high standing in search of truth and understanding.

From that cloud inside we hear the voice of Aristophanes.

ARISTOPHANES: I prefer you to bear, Tellenmagnum, than Socrates. As a man, he is painful to lend an ear.

VINCENT VAN GOGH: I disagree. I lent mine with pleasure in exchange for a picture--a pure treasure.

Heraclitus, the obscure one, now approaches Tellenmagnum, fascinated by his unique entrance.

HERACLITUS: I am that fire that you have omitted from your attire.

TELLENMAGNUM: All parts of all arts are related to the whole, which from inside the Cave they stole.

HERACLITUS: It is in this state of flux, of flow--of becoming something we think we know and don't know, that we see Nature's paradoxical pairs of opposites. If you do not expect the unexpected, you will not find it.

TELLENMAGNUM: Things do not tire in exchange for fire.

HERACLITUS: As an illuminated beast you bear well what you wear. Your range from East to West is the test.

TELLENMAGNUM: In our cave, along with the fire, we had the bow and the lyre.

HERACLITUS: It is the harmony of opposite tensions. Before my liberation, I too was in a kind of hibernation.

TELLENMAGNUM: Long live the sleep of the deep.

SOCRATES: I know something of nothing and nothing of something.

HERACLITUS: I only know the glow.

Coming straight from the cloud inside and directed towards Socrates comes the voice of Aristophanes.

ARISTOPHANES: If I can't pour down my rain then I am in pain.

Eliot scrutinizes Tellenmagnum.

T.S. ELIOT: How do you "bear" the weight of your coat of thick fur?

TELLENMAGNUM: My coat-of-arms hides deep secrets of many charms.

As if things could not get any more bizarre and in stark contrast to Tellenmagnum, a man of small stature appears very nonchalantly at the front door dressed in a wrinkled white suit wearing a tiny white derby hat capping a "great stone face." It is the legendary Buster Keaton! Tellenmagnum wastes no time in picking him up and hurling him through the door where he lands and then slides across the wooden floor.

Keaton gets up quickly, apparently unhurt and looks unmoved after sweeping the floor.

BUSTER KEATON: Always coming out on top, this is why they call me the human mop!

T.S. ELIOT: You are a guy who trained for it all just to know how to take a fall?

Keaton looks at Eliot with his stone face saying nothing, quietly surveying the house as if looking for something. He speaks only mouthing the words as if in a silent movie and we see what he is saying in screen titles.

BUSTER KEATON: I have an idea for the basic story. Let's start shooting. We need no script.

ERIK SATIE: Thus spoke my favorite underdog: the "human mop."

Keaton looks back at Satie with no apparent emotional reaction.

ERIK SATIE: *(Smiling)* Love your poker face--the trademarks of a comedic ace.

T.S. ELIOT: Just with your eyes and expressive body language, you convey your deepest feeling with a sense of profound optimism and perseverance.

Keaton then speaks out directly, not as if in a silent movie.

BUSTER KEATON: For years I was knocked over, thrown through windows, dropped downstairs and essentially used as a living prop--hence my nickname: the "human mop."

ERIK SATIE: In a world that exaggerates everything and overdramatizes every emotion, you remain impassive and solemn with your stone-faced inscrutability as a most powerful potion.

T.S. ELIOT: Buster, you bring positivity with your clever and inquisitive activity.

BUSTER KEATON: Stepping on and off a moving train is as simple for me as getting out of bed. I was told, the subtlety of my work as "physically poetic" could be described as the wit of a stoic.

ERIK SATIE: Weren't you coming with Becket?

BUSTER KEATON: Yes, we did a film together called: "Film."

ERIK SATIE: How was it?

BUSTER KEATON: One of those art things. I was confused when we shot it and am still confused.

T.S. ELIOT: Anyone seen Becket?

ERIK SATIE: No, WE are still waiting. No one can teach anyone what they need or want.

T.S. ELIOT: Go on!

ERIK SATIE: They can only teach what they know. You really just have to go out and do it yourself.

BUSTER KEATON: We are here still waiting for Beckett, and I am sure he is there, somewhere, waiting for us!

Einstein is back at the drawing table hard at work on his "Theory of Everything."

ALBERT EINSTEIN: My name means "one stone" and maybe it is all as simple as that.

TELLENMAGNUM: As what?

ALBERT EINSTEIN: My theory of everything, my unification theory.

TELLENMAGNUM: Our cave was carved out of one stone, where its acoustic space resonated its own inherent tone.

ALBERT EINSTEIN: I'm listening.

TELLENMAGNUM: What we painted on the cave wall reflected what we heard resounding around us all.

ALBERT EINSTEIN: I've always wanted to know God's thoughts in a mathematical way.

TELLENMAGNUM: God thinks in sound and image.

Eliot is in the wings just listening but can't hold back and jumps into the conversation.

T.S. ELIOT: Poetry is not a turning loose of emotion, but an escape from emotion. It is not the expression of personality, but an escape from personality. But of course, only those who have personality and emotions know what it means to want to escape.

ERIK SATIE: Just look at Buster Keaton. His "Great Stone Face" is ideal poetic space.

T.S. ELIOT: Zeuxis stated in 400 BC: "Criticism comes easier than craftsmanship."

ERIK SATIE: Let's all jump aboard this "ship-of-craft."

Samuel Beckett finally makes his much belated appearance.

SAMUEL BECKETT: We are all born mad. Some remain so. I can't go on. I'll go on.

T.S. ELIOT: I love it when you see it stated as simply: don't blame the boot for the fault of the foot.

TELLENMAGNUM: I have come to save what 30,000 years ago we created in a cave.

ERIK SATIE: We are all ears. *(He glances over at Van Gogh.)* Well, almost all.

Beethoven is straining with his ear funnel to hear all that is going on.

LUDWIG VAN BEETHOVEN: What!!!

TELLENMAGNUM: In that acoustic cave what we painted on the wall emanated its own sound call. As start of the very first "temple of art," it was what made space sacred.

Beethoven does not hear Tellenmagnum but understands him intuitively.

LUDWIG VAN BEETHOVEN: I am a slave to my own sound cave. I must compose or will quickly begin to decompose.

Beethoven sings out DA DA DA Dummmm! At the same moment there is another loud knock. It is Voltaire.

T.S. ELIOT: Welcome to our little cocktail affair, Monsieur Voltaire.

Voltaire has officially arrived dressed in dandy white in a fair display of his own jaunty air.

VOLTAIRE: God is a comedian playing to an audience too afraid to laugh.

Keaton just stares at Voltaire with his Great Stone Face and of course says nothing. Voltaire points at Keaton.

VOLTAIRE: Now that is funny!

ERIK SATIE: He is our "human mop"--here to keep our minds clean from bottom to top.

VOLTAIRE: The secret of being a bore is to tell everything.

He looks back at Keaton again noting his stone face.

VOLTAIRE: ...Most interesting man I ever met.

Socrates reappears.

SOCRATES: Besides being a comedian, how would YOU define God?

VOLTAIRE: Judge a man by his questions rather than his answers.

SOCRATES: Didn't you once say: "The ear is the avenue to the heart," or was it "art?"

VOLTAIRE: Either will suffice as it is the ear which is the key device in our struggle to weigh virtue over vice.

Nostradamus, still strolling around, displays his great white robe ostentatiously.

NOSTRADAMUS: I have seen all this come to pass by gazing into my bowl of water made of brass.

SOCRATES: Were you able to clearly see my demise with the help of your magician's disguise?

NOSTRADAMUS: Yes and no. At that precise moment I saw your shroud, which, because of the dim light I mistook for a cloud.

Aristophanes never too far away lets out a raucous laugh.

VOLTAIRE: Never heard a cloud laugh before, but like I said, God is a comedian. I came here to write about your cocktail party.

T.S. ELIOT: We are all here to celebrate.

VOLTAIRE: To hold a pen is to be at war.

ERIK SATIE: We are all in our "battle positions."

Eliot adjusts the angle of his large photo of Groucho Marx on the wall of the main hall.

VOLTAIRE: I have read your poem entitled: "The Triumph of Bullshit."

T.S. ELIOT: Really! I don't know whether to be surprised or excited.

VOLTAIRE: Maybe a little of each. Weren't you the first person to use the term?

T.S. ELIOT: Bullshit?!

VOLTAIRE: You mean it's not true?

Eliot laughs out loud and Aristophanes howls.

ARISTOPHANES: Now you are starting to speak my language.

Keaton, still with his Great Stone face, examines the door frame as if measuring it.

T.S. ELIOT: It has been defined as: To discourse upon the contexts, frames of reference and points of observation which would determine the origin, nature and meaning of data, if one had any.

56

Keaton is now standing in the doorway completely still with his eyes riveted at a single point in the space in front of him.

T.S. ELIOT: My "Road to Damascus" was Harvard to London to Paris...

Eliot's voice drifts off as he is still standing there in his four-piece white suit. Keaton closes his eyes as Satie continues eyeing him.

ERIK SATIE: He imagines staring unblinkingly at the "camera," the front wall of a two-story house crashing down on him. He escapes unhurt because his body is perfectly framed by an open window--or was it a door?

Beckett reappears again looking even more confused.

SAMUEL BECKETT: I just heard that you are still waiting for me. I have been here and am waiting for you to stop waiting for me.

ERIK SATIE: Your "waiting fame" precedes your name in this waiting game.

ALBERT EINSTEIN: This party is moving faster than the "speed of sight," as I get younger by the night.

T.S. ELIOT: Don't you mean "light?"

ALBERT EINSTEIN: Isn't it all relative? Oh...my mistake, I imagined I was a fast-moving train with no brake.

Aristophanes, now getting restless yet fully awake, blasts out some random advice from inside his cloud still invisible to us.

ARISTOPHANES: The secret to a creative mind is a diet that is sparse, and to write a play that is preferably a farce.

On the subject of food and animals, a new arrival appears at the main door of the mansion where we last saw Keaton.

T.S. ELIOT: It must have been a struggle for you to "survive" this storm Mr. Darwin.

CHARLES DARWIN: I can now compete in this test for overall survivor of the fittest.

T.S. ELIOT: We have an open bar but are not serving food, to keep everyone moving in a lighter mood.

CHARLES DARWIN: *(Chuckles)* Then I can only dream of my exotic animals of late, that I not only studied but also ate.

T.S. ELIOT: I have heard of you engorging "strange flesh," when you headed the "Glutton Club" at Cambridge University.

CHARLES DARWIN: *(Laughs again)* Oh, you mean all those owls, hawks, armadillos, giant iguanas and giant tortoises aboard the "Beagle?"

Shaw gets out of his "revolving writing room" and goes over to see Darwin.

GEORGE BERNARD SHAW: While you are preoccupied in how we are all evolving, I have been busy writing in my room slowing revolving.

58

T.S. ELIOT: It might not be food and drink, per se, that fosters creative blenders, but rather, conviviality and intellectual cross-fertilization that a good meal engenders.

SOCRATES: The centerpiece of our city life in Athens was the "symposia," literally: "drinking together." We would spend hours downing diluted wine and discussing philosophy, poetry and the latest gossip, savoring each and every moment down to that last sip.

Straight from the "cloud" Aristophanes "drops" in.

ARISTOPHANES: Even though you, Mr. Eliot, were the first to write the word "bullshit," that "symposia" was the first to practice it!

Aristophanes howls with his own sardonic remark.

Freud is still marauding around high on cocaine and equally high with his fascination for so many "patients" he is dying to treat.

SIGMUND FREUD: My favorite spot to sip my short black coffee was at the "Cafe Laudtmann" in the corner facing outward, ideal for observing the creative milieu unfolding all around in plain view.

Just when we think it can't get much better, J.S. Bach is back!

JOHANN SEBASTIAN BACH: My "Coffee Cantata" is a miniature "comic opera," that amusingly expresses an addiction to coffee.

SIGMUND FREUD: Addiction or a helpful aid to diction and dictation?

JOHANN SEBASTIAN BACH: We first performed it fully staged with costumes at Zimmermann's Coffee House. My favorite lines were: *(Singing)* Ah! How sweet coffee tastes, more delicious than a thousand kisses, milder than muscatel wine. Coffee, I have to have coffee! (He continues singing in German.)

Carl Philipp Emanuel Bach has just arrived during his father's coffee aria. He appears in his neatly groomed white wig, a relaxed white tie and off-white coat with a high collar.

ERIK SATIE: No need of any caffeine as we all weather your impetuous mood swings.

Lightning crackles as Carl Philipp Emanuel Bach tackles the keyboard.

Curious key changes, whiplash stops and starts and deceptive cadences, leaving you wondering if this isn't the musical equivalent of "Attention Deficit Hyperactivity Disorder."

CARL PHILIPP EMANUEL BACH: I am impressed Mr. Satie. You have my personality corralled! I have been called quirky and known to have calculated instability. I love to tease a theme and when I push it around and slice it up, I sometimes even bring it back in the "wrong key."

ERIK SATIE: Yeah, that's the "son." Forward thinking, a glimpse into pure elegance and wit, not looking back to Father Bach nor ever blinking.

CARL PHILIPP EMANUEL BACH: I have always felt underappreciated and of course underpaid, though I kept on with my "sensitive style," through the years with no outside aid.

Over at the bar there is some commotion with Joe and Ernest Hemingway.

JOE: I sometimes think of myself as more of a "bard tender" than a bartender.

ERNEST HEMINGWAY: A man does not exist until he is drunk.

Hemingway suddenly whirls around to the bartender.

ERNEST HEMINGWAY: Another mojito!

JOE: I do a little scribbling myself, Mr. Hemingway.

Hemingway quickly downs the drink and yells out for another.

ERNEST HEMINGWAY: Let's change the subject. I have no advice nor any encouragement for anyone.

JOE: I draw too and play music as well to take some pressure off my writing.

Completely aloof, Hemingway gazes out into the drawing room not listening to the babbling of the bartender.

ERNEST HEMINGWAY: Who is that enormous character all wrapped up in the white polar bear fur?

JOE: Who? Him?...That's Tellenmagnum!

ERNEST HEMINGWAY: Tellen--who?

JOE: Magnum.

ERNEST HEMINGWAY: Now that sounds like some force going all the way back to an original source!

JOE: Back to his "cave" 30,000 years ago!

ERNEST HEMINGWAY: Huh?!

JOE: Word has it he's been in deep hibernation, like some kind of "mythical bear." *(He hesitates.)* But please Sir, hope you're not thinking of shooting him *(He smiles sardonically.)*

Hemingway is obviously taken by Tellenmagnum, mesmerized and lost in thought.

ERNEST HEMINGWAY: Huh? What? Shoot? Shoot who? *(He looks at Tellenmagnum, then laughs.)* My big game days are over. Now it's only the "little game," that distracts me from my lack of writing, that's gone wild and now impossible to tame.

JOE: And?

ERNEST HEMINGWAY: Well, that's the problem. I am used to taking the bull by the horns both figuratively AND literally. *(He laughs deeply.)* Another mojito!

Hemingway slams the empty glass down on the bar.

Tellenmagnum feels Hemingway's glare and glances in his direction. Darwin then turns to Eliot.

CHARLES DARWIN: Just looking at that "beast" over there makes my mouth water.

Eliot stares back at Darwin both a little shocked and upset.

T.S. ELIOT: You referring to our honored guest, Tellenmagnum?

CHARLES DARWIN: Oh, it's got a name? *(He laughs.)*

T.S. ELIOT: What's the matter with you. You are not behaving yourself. I was expecting something more "evolved" from you.

CHARLES DARWIN: In Galapagos, I rode tortoises and drank fluid from their bladders. On the Beagle, we ate their flesh along with puma flesh that tasted a bit like veal.

T.S. ELIOT: This is London, Charles. Stop hallucinating about that ideal meal you once shared of crusted crustacea, mollusca salad, primordial soup and hunter-gatherer pie.

TELLENMAGNUM: Why do I feel as though the eyes of a dangerous hunter has set his sights on me?

Voltaire, who has been chatting with Tellenmagnum, is now obviously fascinated with the dynamic of the drawing room as he looks over at the bar.

VOLTAIRE: There's that writer named Hemingway. He wrote an interesting and Zen-like short work called: "The Nick Adams Stories." He then, well, went on to win the Nobel Prize, I recall reading somewhere.

TELLENMAGNUM: Nobel? What's that?

Darwin then looks over at Eliot and smiles, still fascinated with Tellenmagnum.

CHARLES DARWIN: Could he be my missing link, if he is in fact whom I think?

T.S. ELIOT: Missing? You're crazy Darwin. He is here, right in front of you!

CHARLES DARWIN: Without that link, my theory remains just that-- an incomplete evolution of man's history.

Hemingway moves closer to Tellenmagnum to get a better look. Joe, the bartender, seems somewhat relieved that he has moved on. He now mutters to himself and out loud.

JOE: Who knows what guest will cross that threshold next?

Outside in front of the mansion there is some more commotion as Nietzsche has run over to Shakespeare's horse to stop a passerby from striking it.

FRIEDRICH NIETZSCHE: How could you hit that innocent horse. I should beat your skull in for that!

Nietzsche then falls to the ground and weeps uncontrollably. Beethoven yells into the wind, then walks over to the bent over Nietzsche and helps him up.

LUDWIG VAN BEETHOVEN: Come inside and I'll play something for you.

64

Beethoven escorts him back inside the mansion. As they enter, they witness another guest just arriving on the scene. No one has a clear idea just who it is as he approaches the door walking with difficulty in an old- fashioned deep-sea diving suit. His breathing is obviously labored beneath this heavy cumbersome suit. Eliot opens the door and stares in disbelief at the figure in front of him.

SALVADOR DALI: I live at the bottom of the "Sea of Unconsciousness!"

Eliot immediately notices how Dali is struggling to even breathe and calls Satie for help.

T.S. ELIOT: Satie! Give me a hand here!

Satie arrives and they are both together able to pull off the underwater heavy helmet. Now Eliot sees the iconic mustache and immediately recognizes who it is.

T.S. ELIOT: Dali!

ERIK SATIE: Salvador! The "savior" himself! My church is now saved.

Dali now breathes deeply, desperate for air, literally gulping it in.

SALVADOR DALI: Do you have any cauliflower?

ERIK SATIE: Cauliflower? And they call me weird!

SALVADOR DALI: I desperately need to see and appreciate its logarithmic curve. Look over there at my white Rolls Royce!

Both Eliot and Satie turn to the vehicle and immediately notice it filled with cauliflower!

ERIK SATIE: Did you bring a painting?

SALVADOR DALI: Why yes, that one over there!

T.S. ELIOT: There has already been quite a "buzz" surrounding it.

SALVADOR DALI: Doesn't surprise me. I mixed the paint with the venom of a million wasps.

As soon as Dali gets out of that underwater gear, he finds a not so quiet corner and went into a headstand wearing just his white long underwear. Tellenmagnum, who had been watching this whole "Dali Show," looks over at him standing on his head.

TELLENMAGNUM: That particular show is great to re-invigorate the blood flow!

From his upside-down perspective Dali looks over at Tellenmagnum decked out in his polar bear fur.

SALVADOR DALI: Please ask me why I do this!

TELLENMAGNUM: Go ahead and tell me why.

SALVADOR DALI: It's my way to get a fresh batch of ideas in this semi-lucid state.

T.S. ELIOT: I once saw your "Royal Heart" "beating" together with its amazing 42 rubies, 42 diamonds and two emeralds.

SALVADOR DALI: To get it sold after I drafted it, I had it crafted from pure gold.

Freud lights up another cigar with his brain still afire from cocaine. Thinking profoundly, he puffs out a cloud of white smoke, takes another deep drag on his beloved cigar and quietly savors his dopamine high and state of euphoria from the previous drug. In the meantime, Dali has come down from his headstand and bumps into Freud.

SIGMUND FREUD: If I could have you around all the time, I wouldn't need any...

SALVADOR DALI: ...of the "other" drugs. Thanks for the compliment. You must know that I self-medicate with "myself."

SIGMUND FREUD: I envy that in you.

SALVADOR DALI: My goal is to live in my own subconscious world.

SIGMUND FREUD: I admit I once took you for a fool, before becoming aware of your subconscious pool.

SALVADOR DALI: You are the Father of that Subconscious World where I used to dive into to thrive, and as an artist hope to survive.

Dali presents Freud with a plaster sculpture of his brain.

SALVADOR DALI: You might be able to make some sense out of this where others could not.

SIGMUND FREUD: It looks to be roughly the same size as Einstein's, but the surface folds are slightly different.

Freud continues closely examining this replica of Dali's brain.

SALVADOR DALI: The brain is an organ of the mind. Since I am out of my mind I can now get a more objective view of it.

Hearing his name come up in the conversation, Einstein, himself, goes over to where to two are conversing.

ALBERT EINSTEIN: My ideas on space and time came in a flash and not over the space of time. I did not come up with the "continuum" in a "vacuum."

SALVADOR DALI: Doing my "headstand" helps me understand where I stand, balancing using the hand.

Beethoven is over at the harpsichord and starts playing for Nietzsche to calm him down after that horse incident. Lewis Carroll strains his ear to be able to hear.

LEWIS CARROLL: I-I-I-Lo-Lo Love this!

Beethoven looks up at Carroll straining to hear sensing he is obviously deaf in one ear.

LUDWIG VAN BEETHOVEN: Right or left?

LEWIS CARROLL: Left!

LUDWIG VAN BEETHOVEN: Good. We all hear better with our right anyway.

At the door now is a crazed looking man who has arrived in a Troika, parked just behind Shakespeare's horse. It is none other than Fyodor Dostoevsky.

FYODOR DOSTOEVSKY: Not even sure if I am supposed to be here. I got a letter in St. Petersburg hand-delivered by a horseman. I came here through the underground network and wrote some notes along the way.

He holds up a stack of scribblings on some badly wrinkled pages. Now inside, over at the harpsichord, Beethoven stops to speak to Carroll.

LUDWIG VAN BEETHOVEN: I make use of your "Nyctograph" device nightly. It has saved me, especially while writing the Ninth.

LEWIS CARROLL: You-you-you nnnnnn-ote your-your ideas.

Beethoven can't hide his discomfort with all of Carroll's stammering.

LUDWIG VAN BEETHOVEN: Yesss! At night, in the dark without getting out of bed.

LEWIS CARROLL: FFFFFFantastic.

Dostoevsky hurries over to a wall that is somewhat empty, except for that large photo of Groucho Marx, which he immediately takes down. He quickly pulls out a stick of dark charcoal to start writing on that huge blank wall space. Eliot sees what he is doing and is shocked.

T.S. ELIOT: Fyodor, my friend, what on earth?

Dostoevsky is writing like a man "possessed."

FYODOR DOSTOEVSKY: My new novel cannot wait. My anti-hero, Stavrogin, is speaking to me again, asking to be resurrected.

Eliot doesn't get in his way but does glance again at that large photo of Groucho now resting on the floor and smiles wryly.

T.S. ELIOT: By all means let him speak out. The fate of that character is hanging in balance no matter where or how he shows up. The most sincere and astute people always surrounded Groucho with reverence and admiration.

Recognizing the immense presence of Dostoevsky, Beethoven stops playing hoping the crisis with Nietzsche and the horse has passed.

LUDWIG VAN BEETHOVEN: Through my "dark spiritual night," you were my one guiding light. We all pass through our own personal "firing squads," then, surviving, go on to do our best work. Thank you!

FYODOR DOSTOEVSKY: I had a custom-made extra-large closet in St. Petersburg with your music constantly playing in my mind whenever I went into it to meditate and be alone.

LUDWIG VAN BEETHOVEN: That is impressive.

FYODOR DOSTOEVSKY: One can know a man from his laugh, and if you like a man's laugh before you know anything of him, you may confidently say that he is a good man.

LUDWIG VAN BEETHOVEN: Once deprived of doing our own work we go mad!

FYODOR DOSTOEVSKY: Stark-raving mad!!

Suddenly Dostoevsky leaves Beethoven and hurries over to the bar and quickly asks Joe for a shot of cognac. Then turns back to Eliot to ask.

FYODOR DOSTOEVSKY: I expect we should be served some dessert soon?

T.S. ELIOT: There is no food available, Fyodor. We mentioned that in the invitation we sent you.

FYODOR DOSTOEVSKY: That is a small tragedy. I am now imagining a hearty soup made from broth, finely sliced sausage, sauerkraut and pickles, veal escalope and "rastegai."

T.S. ELIOT: Rastegai?

FYODOR DOSTOEVSKY: Baked pies with an opening at the top and different fillings.

JOE: Mr. Dostoevsky! Can I offer you a shot of grain vodka? Homemade, wheat-based, just like I heard you love?

FYODOR DOSTOEVSKY: What time is it? I usually have that with my breakfast along with some brown bread to chew--that's the best way to drink it.

T.S. ELIOT: As one talented neurotic to another, how do you drink your tea?

FYODOR DOSTOEVSKY: Using my own teaspoon with two lumps of sugar.

Charles Dickens now comes as Dostoevsky immediately recognizes him.

FYODOR DOSTOEVSKY: Charles, whether you know or not, you have enriched my imagination, especially regarding your psychological conceptions.

CHARLES DICKENS: Thanks--your characters are much more complicated and existentially desperate.

Dickens has already taken out his comb again and keeps running it through his hair as the two continue talking.

CHARLES DICKENS: I am in the process of cleaning and rearranging this drawing room. would you like to help?

Distracted now, Dostoevsky doesn't even hear Dickens as he suddenly has turned back to his writing wall.

FYODOR DOSTOEVSKY: Stavrogin is speaking through me. Got to get this out and down.

CHARLES DICKENS: On "my walls?"

FYODOR DOSTOEVSKY: Yours?!

CHARLES DICKENS: Yes! I am going to put some shelves here with fake books!

FYODOR DOSTOEVSKY: Fake?! And they call me crazy!

Arriving now as the storm rages on is Alexander Pushkin, the great Romantic, Russian poet and writer. He is wearing a white coat to accompany blond-dyed hair in striking contrast to his dark Ethiopian skin color. He has a white-handled gun in his hand fresh from his most recent duel. This is enough to pull Dostoevsky away from Stavrogin and his wall once more.

FYODOR DOSTOEVSKY: How many are you up to now, my dear Alex?

ALEXANDER PUSHKIN: Nearly twenty, I guess, of my own challenges, while I have received seven from others. Four actually took place.

FYODOR DOSTOEVSKY: It is widely known you are an expert marksman.

ALEXANDER PUSHKIN: But my deadly aim is not nearly as sharp as the fame your pen can claim.

FYODOR DOSTOEVSKY: How could you be with that beauty, Natalya, who is without a brain, a soul, a heart, or talent, just naked beauty, striking yes, in a word, like a sword?

ALEXANDER PUSHKIN: Whenever I make a hormonal decision, I always have a puncher's chance.

FYODOR DOSTOEVSKY: Most duels are fought at a distance of 25 to 30 steps but you...

ALEXANDER PUSHKIN: Agreed to one of ten steps. Yes! I am an insane poet!

FYODOR DOSTOEVSKY: You now are Mother Russia's favorite son. It's definitely not myself nor Tolstoy, who write classic drama under the backdrop of a Slavic sky.

T.S. ELIOT: Pushkin! They say you are their everything. The Russians believe that you accompany them in everything they say and think.

ALEXANDER PUSHKIN: Speaking of thinking, I need a shot of vodka. No need for it to be grain and nothing to explain.

T.S. ELIOT: Go on...

ALEXANDER PUSHKIN: I am Russia's first and only Black poet, descended from an Ethiopian prisoner who somehow became Peter the Great's favorite advisor.

Shakespeare has now made his reappearance after going outside to check on the emotional state of his horse.

SHAKESPEARE: You are known for your temper and love of women, as well as being a skillful master of the modern Russian language.

ALEXANDER PUSHKIN: Both you and I can assume any shape that the outside world can offer.

SHAKESPEARE: We are protean, unable to draw the world into ourselves, so we strive to maintain its multitude of shapes and forms outside the brain.

Aristophanes lets out another burst of laughter from up in his protective cloud.

ARISTOPHANES: There is no doubt as to who Pushkin is, but your identity is still a bit cloudy. I know much about anything nebulous.

He laughs again long and hard as Socrates in his white toga ambles back on in.

SOCRATES: As long as he stays in the clouds, he can do no harm. I do worry, though, when he decides to let loose his rain of frogs and deadly swarms of wasps.

Dostoevsky continues on with charcoal writing on Eliot's clean white wall, completely ignoring Dickens's pleas.

FYODOR DOSTOEVSKY: What a joy it is to write with emotion in Russian. It has everything great literature craves: strength of expression, rich vocabulary, vast arsenal of adjectives, epithets, descriptions, figures of speech, musicality, tenderness and rhythm.

ALEXANDER PUSHKIN: And much more suited for literature, art and poetry than for doing business.

T.S. ELIOT: I would have to agree. English is more practical, based on verbs--a language of doing.

FYODOR DOSTOEVSKY: Exactly! Russian is based more on nouns and adjectives. It loves its participle construction and long sentences.

ALEXANDER PUSHKIN: Being clearly excessive, good for description and contemplation, it is the perfect expression of the Russian character.

FYODOR DOSTOEVSKY: We are more engrossed in thought rather than action.

Aristophanes is still speaking from his cloud as he shouts out to Shakespeare.

ARISTOPHANES: "To be or not to be," that is still your question, Sir William. What will it be?

SHAKESPEARE: For me, you are unbidden for as long as you choose to remain hidden, just a disembodied voice clamoring for attention by your own choice.

Aristophanes yells down to Joe, the bartender.

ARISTOPHANES: Quickly, bring me a beaker of wine, so that I may wet my mind and say something clever, remaining up here quiet will not happen, never.

SOCRATES: It was not me but Plato's student, Aristotle, who once spouted: "No great genius has ever existed without some touch of madness."

ARISTOPHANES: You will never make the crab walk straight.

SHAKESPEARE: That is no headline to grab but a "sideline" of the crab.

Surprisingly, Becket is back and ready to mount his attack.

SAMUEL BECKETT: We are all born mad. Some remain so.

Van Gogh, in a hurry, runs into the main hallway, where Dostoevsky is scribbling on the wall and yells out.

VINCENT VAN GOGH: I captured her. I finished that last "potato-eater." My painting is now complete. Emilie du Chatelet, as Muse, provided me with that final inspirational moment to use.

Van Gogh turns to Mr. Dickens.

VINCENT VAN GOGH: And you, my English friend, put that final spell on her. Thank you, thank you!

George Sand is back displaying her elegant white tuxedo and white top hat with accompanying stylish white cane brandishing it for all to see.

GEORGE SAND: This is for sure not the blind person's cane, nor is it a seer's magical "weathervane." It is never implemented to guide but as an accessory helping me to hide.

Balzac returns, having consumed more coffee together with Bach at the coffee bar. It had been set up alongside the regular bar where Joe is able to man them both.

HONORÉ DE BALZAC: Madame Sand, you are a "writing animal" in a titanium shawl, who could take us all down in a page quantity brawl.

GEORGE SAND: You think so?

HONORÉ DE BALZAC: Yes! We are all amazed at your ability to knock out twenty pages at a stretch in any circumstance, any time of day or night.

Sand takes a deep puff on her cigar and blows it Balzac's way.

GEORGE SAND: Don't get carried away Monsieur Balzac! I am a writing whore; I do it to not become a complete bore.

T.S. ELIOT: You have boldly assumed the right to behave as a man by doing it as overpoweringly and unscrupulously as you can.

GEORGE SAND: Then, just call me a phenomenon and not a writer aspiring to amass a canon.

ERIK SATIE: I assume, Madame Sand, that you are your own guest, forever embarking on "his" or "her" identity test.

GEORGE SAND: A truth unbroken and clearly well-spoken.

Nostradamus is back in his corner staring into his brass bowl full of water. He raises his arms as if ready to proclaim a new reading, sighting or prophetic vision.

NOSTRADAMUS: Though clearly not a patrician, he is without a doubt a great mathematician. Besides knowing geometry, he became the pillar of trigonometry. Considered to be one of history's many guides, he is the sum of the square of his two other sides.

It is Pythagoras, who is at this moment approaching his targeted "station," which he found by implementing triangulation. His new angle provides the party at Eliot's mansion with another mystery to untangle.

PYTHAGORAS: I finally decided to come when I heard you were not serving any white beans. I got here trekking cross country, following the sun's rays to avoid walking on any of the highways.

T.S. ELIOT: Pythagoras, who was your muse when you came up with your square of the hypotenuse?

PYTHAGORAS: Geometry is my god, which is why it has been called "Sacred Geometry." It comes down to approaching it at the right angle.

T.S. ELIOT: You are definitely not full of beans. *(He laughs lightly.)*

PYTHAGORAS: *(Angrily)* I would do nothing for beans!

T.S. ELIOT: No offense, just a little joke.

Aristophanes yells out from inside the cloud inside the mansion.

ARISTOPHANES: You are all broke, and none can even take a little joke. I am the funny one, though I look at you square, there is still nothing I can square.

Pythagoras stoically ignores this frivolous bantering.

PYTHAGORAS: All natural phenomena I can explain mathematically.

Einstein hears the word "mathematics" and swings around to join in.

ALBERT EINSTEIN: Thank you for paving the way for the study of Physics. I owe my entire life to you.

PYTHAGORAS: Excuse me, do we know each other, maybe a relative?

ALBERT EINSTEIN: Aren't we all? Isn't everything?

PYTHAGORAS: I do know we are both pacifists.

Aristophanes comes back from the cloud to counter Pythagoras.

ARISTOPHANES: Now that is funny. Your message suffered greatly after you died in a fight!

PYTHAGORAS: Died!?

ARISTOPHANES: You were able to make it here because of your belief in reincarnation.

Suddenly, there is a deep growl outside in the storm in front of the mansion. Tellenmagnum, who was nearest to the front door, flings it open and is met face to face with a large polar bear on his hind legs pawing at the door to be let in. Seeing Tellenmagnum wearing polar bear furs, he calms a little as if recognizing a possible relative.

TELLENMAGNUM: Give me some skin, my brother. We are true soulmates.

Tellenmagnum quickly examines the bear's keeper alongside it and looks around to call for Eliot to come. Hurrying to the door,

Eliot immediately recognizes his old friend, Lord Byron. They hug emotionally.

LORD BYRON: It's alright. He is actually quite friendly. I have had him since my days at Cambridge!

T.S. ELIOT: Your "Don Juan" persona precedes you--another living legend to join our little Cocktail Party.

LORD BYRON: No one could "bear" it when I got him enrolled at the university. It is of course not true when Lady Caroline referred to me as "mad, bad and dangerous."

T.S. ELIOT: You, of course not, the bear, maybe.

ERIK SATIE: You and your beast of a guest look as though you are both in need of some rest. Tellenmagnum, could you give us a hand?

Tellenmagnum takes the now calmer polar bear out behind to the back shed of the mansion. Satie pulls Eliot aside to talk privately.

ERIK SATIE: Where do you keep your shotguns you usually carry on those fox hunts?

T.S. ELIOT: On the wall in my study.

ERIK SATIE: Should we lock them up before Hemingway gets any wild ideas?

T.S. ELIOT: Brilliant, yes of course. Where is he now?

ERIK SATIE: Still at the bar nursing his umpteenth mojito!

Joe, the bartender is mumbling to himself.

JOE: How do I get this beaker of wine Aristophanes ordered up to his cloud?

Hemingway is still methodically downing mojitos at Joe's bar.

ERNEST HEMINGWAY: I thought I just heard a deep growl.

JOE: Growl? Here?!

ERNEST HEMINGWAY: Must be hallucinating...you asked me earlier about writing tips, Here's one! Just don't talk about it to anyone! Don't think about it after you stop for the day.

JOE: That's good to know!

ERNEST HEMINGWAY: Talking or worrying takes off whatever butterflies have on their wings that helps them take flight.

Now the growling is more intense, louder than ever.

ERNEST HEMINGWAY: I definitely felt that no matter how many mojitos are under my belt. Maybe a bear? I know my wild beasts.

JOE: Bear? Here?

Satie and Eliot have hurried into his study to where the shotguns are racked on the wall.

ERIK SATIE: Hide 'em?

T.S. ELIOT: By all means! Hemingway is beyond drunk by now.

Tellenmagnum has already taken Lord Byron's bear through the hallway to the back of the mansion. Hemingway catches a glimpse of them as they pass in front of the drawing room's open double doors.

ERNEST HEMINGWAY: Look! A polar bear! What did I tell you. And now I am just drunk enough to snag me a bear skin for my Cuban hideaway lodge!

Hemingway stumbles after the disappearing bear. On his way out he runs into both Satie and Eliot loaded down with shotguns. Instinctively, he rips one out of Satie's white-knuckled hands and goes after the bear. In this confusion Eliot spots Gauguin close by.

T.S. ELIOT: Quickly Paul, help us restrain Hemingway. He'll shoot Lord Byron's bear if we don't stop him.

They both rush after Hemingway. Suddenly we hear a shot coming from behind the mansion. When they get there, they see Tellenmagnum easily wrestling a very drunk Hemingway to the ground. Tellenmagnum growls at him.

TELLENMAGNUM: Why would you try to kill my "brother?"

Hemingway breaks free of the stranglehold and gasps for air.

ERNEST HEMINGWAY: Brother?!

TELLENMAGNUM: We were "wearing" a similar skin! You couldn't see that?

ERNEST HEMINGWAY: Well...yes...I do now. Who are YOU?

TELLENMAGNUM: Right now, your own worst nightmare!

ERNEST HEMINGWAY: This is definitely not that happy safari ending like the ones I went on in Africa.

TELLENMAGNUM: This is reality! I am the "cave artist" from 30,000 years ago, who was called to come here as a special guest back from my primordial "vision quest."

Eliot and Gauguin arrived just after the shot went off.

TELLENMAGNUM: I grabbed the rifle just as it went off. We are all very lucky. Who is this mad man, by the way?

Tellenmagnum gestures and glowers at Hemingway. Gauguin responds quite facetiously.

PAUL GAUGUIN: That "Great White Hunter!"

Now it is Hemingway's turn to growl.

ERNEST HEMINGWAY: And now one, not so great, but very drunk white writer.

Gauguin helps him up, puts his arm around him as they both head back to the bar for a very much needed drink.

PAUL GAUGUIN: Absinthe!

ERNEST HEMINGWAY: Same. No, not absinthe. Same as before.

Gauguin quickly changes the subject to ease the tension and relax Hemingway.

PAUL GAUGUIN: You know I am Tahiti-bound again. It's in the blood.

ERNEST HEMINGWAY: Know that feeling!

They both toast together as Joe stands by to refill when needed. In the middle of all this excitement they have been "bearing," Henry Miller makes his entrance on a white bicycle wearing his customary short- brimmed hat off to the side, also white. He dismounts his bicycle and "glides" into the hallway, heading straight for Joe and the bar.

HENRY MILLER: Water! Water!

He downs huge gulps then asks Joe for more.

HENRY MILLER: This is how "I" get drunk.

Now he starts whirling around the hall imitating being on a pair of roller skates.

HENRY MILLER: Finally free from June, I can now sing a different tune.

T.S. ELIOT: Glad to see you, "Man of the Tropics!"

HENRY MILLER: My destination has never been a place but rather a new way of looking at things throughout all space.

ERIK SATIE: And your guest?

HENRY MILLER: Oh, you mean Anais? She'll be coming along. She's in the middle of a dream in Paris.

ERIK SATIE: More water?

HENRY MILLER: Yes, I get literally drunk on it all the time.

T.S. ELIOT: Why did you ever decide to expatriate?

HENRY MILLER: Any man serious about being an artist should leave America...and I took my own advice seriously.

T.S. ELIOT: You returned, though and you still feel a foreigner, right?

HENRY MILLER: Yes, my readers are far more interested in that sensational part of my life than the path to individual and spiritual freedom.

T.S. ELIOT: You have always claimed that in order to ascend to that ethereal realm of angels a descent into the dark depths of the soul must precede it from all angles.

HENRY MILLER: It was actually watercolor painting that saved my mind during those turbulent years in Paris.

T.S. ELIOT: I remember you quoted St. Francis once, what was it, do you remember?

HENRY MILLER: "Don't change the world, change worlds." I'm a living contradiction. I agreed to that long ago. I live in chaos, swimming in it. I'm afloat and astray and thinking a million thoughts that are contradictory. I love disorder!

Joe, the bartender brings Miller more water, ironically, feeding the "flame." Beethoven returns singing in a deep voice the theme from his Ninth: "Ode to Joy." Beethoven gesticulates now even more wildly and laughs out loud, while Aristophanes responds from the protective harbor of his cloud.

ARISTOPHANES: A man after my own heart.

Dickens returns to the hall still worried about Dostoevsky writing on "his" clean wall and heads to the bar.

JOE: Why so down Mr. Dickens?

CHARLES DICKENS: I fall into a deep state of depression with the start of each new novel. My mood will gradually lift until I get into a kind of mania near the end.

JOE: Sounds brutal! What is "Charles" up to? "He" has been trying to avoid any conversation since he got here.

Dickens had a mania for referring to himself in third person.

CHARLES DICKENS: "He" has a severe case of agoraphobia.

Suddenly, whirling across the hall, an amazing dancer performs gigantic leaps as part of a very intricate choreography. Miller turns immediately recognizing this movement genius.

HENRY MILLER: Nijinsky! I read his diary so many times I have it almost committed it to memory. He would go weeks speaking only with his body.

Freud also watches him dance.

SIGMUND FREUD: It's called schizophrenia.

Nijinsky does some magnificent pirouettes in the air and now catches the attention of Tellenmagnum, who has by now returned from the back of the mansion with his newfound friend, Lord Byron's polar bear.

TELLENMAGNUM: That whirling dancer is pure inspiration.

He sees Buster Keaton next to him and reaches out picking him up like a small child. Suddenly, he tosses Keaton to the polar bear, who catches Keaton and growls. Keaton looks up at the polar bear's face with his iconic stone expression firmly intact. Tellenmagnum nods to the bear to toss him back, which he does.

TELLENMAGNUM: This "human mop" is as light as a spinning top.

Then, Tellenmagnum literally throws Keaton out the front door now wide open where he softly lands in the strong arms of Heraclitus, who happened to be standing on the front porch getting some air, mentally preparing to light his giant torch. The sage, Heraclitus turned around just at the right moment to catch this "air-borne package." The two now stare at each other with similar stoic expressions.

BUSTER KEATON: I can't say I am not enjoying the moment since I can't be thrown into the same arms twice, which would somehow compromise virtue with vice.

HERACLITUS: I can't argue with that as it does sound quite familiar.

Back inside, Tellenmagnum has taken control of the energized atmosphere after seeing Nijinsky and tossing around Keaton.

TELLENMAGNUM: It is now time to tell our story, or really, my story. What was it that made us so brave to create everything we did inside that prehistoric cave?

Heraclitus returns back inside still carrying Keaton and finally puts him down. Keaton stares at Tellenmagnum with rapt attention.

HERACLITUS: Please continue!

TELLENMAGNUM: Due to the higher functioning of our execution, accompanied by an increase in brain size, especially the neocortex, we created our story on those cave walls.

HERACLITUS: Which you have brought to show us?

TELLENMAGNUM: As you, yourself said about "change," it is the only thing that doesn't change, freely moving outside a more familiar range.

HERACLITUS: Epiphanies abounded and challenges overcome, bringing me to this moment well-rounded.

TELLENMAGNUM: What I painted on the wall was an innate part of my psyche not viewable to all yet obviously a unique adventure for all.

Henry Miller had always been a huge fan of those cave paintings by Tellenmagnum.

HENRY MILLER: They were an inspiration for watercolor pieces I am still working on.

Tellenmagnum picks up a huge brush nearly the size of Buster Keaton's head as Eliot makes a general announcement.

T.S. ELIOT: Consider this mansion, my home, as our own inmost cave here in the very heart of London's "new wave."

At that exact moment, Satie opens the mansion door once more to welcome Antonin Artaud.

ERIK SATIE: Monsieur Artaud, what a timely surprise. Welcome to "Creator's Cave."

ANTONIN ARTAUD: Cave!? That is where I am the most like a knave. Just as Plato urged us to go out of the "cave of shadows" to meet reality, I urge you to stay in the cave to create your "meadows."

T.S. ELIOT: You are on, Monsieur Artaud! Make us feel your theater of The Ordeal!

ANTONIN ARTAUD: First let me present Jerzy Grotowski, my guest, whom I brought in his "holy actor" form.

JERZY GROTOWSKI: We bring to you no tricks, just ourselves laid bare before you as who we really are.

Surprisingly, the polar bear motions to Tellenmagnum with his great paw, indicating for him to meet behind the mansion.

TELLENMAGNUM: Mr. Eliot, does your mansion have a secret, hidden corral where we can go to perform an ancient art ritual.

He looks over at the bear still motioning to him.

T.S. ELIOT: I guess it would be my riding stables where all of our fox-hunting horses are kept.

TELLENMAGNUM: Sounds like an ideal set for us to determine just what to reveal. Now we can discover what has been hidden for so long in that cave, so long forbidden.

HERACLITUS: What fun--we are most nearly ourselves when the seriousness of a child at play has begun.

T.S. ELIOT: What did you once say about "hidden harmony?'

HERACLITUS: Only that it is better than obvious.

ANTONIN ARTAUD: Let's all be athletes of the heart--the pure essence of art.

JERZY GROTOWSKI: We all seek a poetic state, to light a fire in this "cave" to illuminate its gate.

In one bounding lope followed by Tellenmagnum, Lord Byron's polar bear growls on his hind legs as he is the first to get to the stable's rustic sanctum. Eliot flings open the stable doors and releases his three white horses, with their ivory mane, snowy in full blown vane.

ANTONIN ARTAUD: The truth of life lies in the impulsiveness of matter. The mind of men has been poisoned by concepts. Do not ask him only to be cool, to believe that he has found his place in a random psalm--only the madman is truly calm.

TELLENMAGNUM: Let's create!!

He raises up his gigantic, long brush and begins, clearly in no rush.

TELLENMAGNUM: By the way, who brought this pigment "ocher?" I feel right at home inside this warm yet darkened dome.

T.S. ELIOT: Gauguin! He brought it back from Tahiti. He said they used it there to do their bamboo paintings.

Not wanting to miss a moment, Gauguin made his way back to the stables of the tall mansion with no gables.

PAUL GAUGUIN: It is a form of iron oxide. Though the color of rust, it is anything but rusty and made to trace lines of an ancient race.

Van Gogh is also there to watch Tellenmagnum perform his magic. Even Aristophanes, from his "cloud," can see the stable wall through the open doors.

ARISTOPHANES: Look at that explosion of talent, like a cloudburst of rain with fluid content.

The large fire proves to be enough to illuminate the wall where the artist is at work. Everyone is back there in the stable, even Hemingway bringing his freshly made mojito to help dull the pain continually throbbing in his brain.

ARISTOPHANES: All is water!

HERACLITUS: The thunderbolt steers all.

92

Outside there is another crash of lightning as Tellenmagnum applies his red ochre to the wall.

TELLENMAGNUM: Our art is neither Western nor Eastern, not from the North nor South--not earthbound, and clearly driven by sound.

Lord Byron's bear has now calmed down and is softly growling near the fire.

TELLENMAGNUM: It is primordial and arose at the same time as the sun dial. It is our wakeup call being reborn here inside a simple stable stall.

PAUL GAUGUIN: The body of a woman one paints relies on similar traits common to all saints. Look at the water that flows from her arms, breasts and uterus--never rests, always flowing from them to us.

In zen-like economy Tellenmagnum did his sketch in minutes--a genuine masterpiece of primordial symbology.

VINCENT VAN GOGH: I see a large abstract "bear," like the constellation "Ursa Major." It was always in my mind when I painted my "Starry Night."

TELLENMAGNUM: These are stars I have painted just like Vincent said. And here is the "Big Dipper," inside the bear.

The polar bear, and now, friend of Tellenmagnum, appears to be transfixed seeing this image.

TELLENMAGNUM: This is how we used to navigate before my long "drawn out" hibernation.

Van Gogh turns to Gauguin.

VINCENT VAN GOGH: You see a woman in everything. All that water you imagined is still contained in "Ursa Major..."

ANTONIN ARTAUD: The Great Bear.

HERACLITUS: It was one of the constellations catalogued by the Greek astronomer, Ptolemy, in the second century.

SOCRATES: It is also associated with Callisto, a nymph turned into a bear by Zeus's jealous wife, Hera.

VINCENT VAN GOGH: There is your woman and muse, Paul--Callisto, the nymph.

PAUL GAUGUIN: I usually "see" what is hidden.

ANTONIN ARTAUD: Callisto lived as a bear for the next fifteen years.

Tellenmagnum glances over at his polar bear friend.

ANTONIN ARTAUD: ...roaming the forest and always running and hiding from hunters.

JERZY GROTOWSKI: In the Hindu legend, the brightest stars of Ursa Major represent the Seven Sages and the constellation known as "Saptarchi." In some Native American tales, the bowl of the "Big Dipper" represents a large bear and the stars that mark the handle are the warrior chasing it. Since the constellation is pretty low in the sky in autumn, the legend says that it is the blood of the wounded bear that causes the leaves to turn red.

TELLENMAGNUM: Like I just said, this is how we used to navigate since it points to the North Star, Polaris.

The polar bear is now moving his head and it appears as though he is nodding.

ANTONIN ARTAUD: We have entered shaman's territory in this part of our story. I have seen wild horses racing through the air like distant meteors, lovers separated by hurricanes and a celestial storm where planets collide.

Quiet for long enough, Freud now seizes his moment to express himself.

SIGMUND FREUD: You appear, as poets do, to easily fall through mirrors into the subconscious, or into an equally altered state.

ANTONIN ARTAUD: It could be our natural state, this "inmost cave," that if not explored and known, could close up, sealing our fate.

TELLENMAGNUM: I am the gate to this shift from outward to inward.

ANTONIN ARTAUD: Yes! A whole new language seems to be needed to be invented. I envision actors in geometric robes living as moving hieroglyphs.

JERZY GROTOWSKI: We are all here as both actors AND spectators.

T.S. ELIOT: That was exactly my idea for this "Cocktail Party."

Anais Nin literally bursts onto the scene and immediately spots both Artaud and Miller. Keaton is also around, in and out of the cave. Artaud is still fascinated by Keaton.

ANTONIN ARTAUD: Just like they have always said: this human mop is as light as a top.

Both Keaton and Artaud give each other their own version of that "deadpan stare," each trying to make the other laugh. Miller ultimately interrupts their little contest.

HENRY MILLER: Whoever can enact "the plague" as well as you will never need a contract. To purge is to be protected from its surge.

ANAIS NIN: *(Speaking to Miller)* I imagined seeing you in a purple robe but instead you are all in white like a cloud encircling a globe.

TELLENMAGNUM: Here, ancient secrets have been revealed as these forces of the cosmos align for us what has congealed. No longer are we confused while here in this cave with our new being suddenly fused.

Miller and Anais Nin embrace warmly.

HENRY MILLER: I am back and still smoldering with passion, like smoking wine straight from the vine. Not a passion just for flesh, but a devouring hunger for us to mesh.

ANAIS NIN: Everyone seems to have their brakes on...I never feel the brakes. I overflow. And when I feel your excitement about life flaring next to mine, it makes me dizzy to tread that line nearly invisible being so fine.

HENRY MILLER: I am continually on the verge of getting up and throwing my arms around you.

The polar bear leaves the warmth of the fire and comes over to stand next to his friend, Tellenmagnum.

TELLENMAGNUM: We are both of the "same skin" and have nothing to "hide." Our camouflage is white, symbolizing surrender. We understand our need to adapt and the will to survive in the harshest of lands. Accepting the surrounding we belong here in this cave abounding.

The polar bear stares at Tellenmagnum, then at the diminutive Keaton, and then over at Artaud.

TELLENMAGNUM: I can read your thoughts and plans; you ARE that white flag in a long process over time to become master like the winter stag.

The polar bear stretches out his long arm and huge paw.

TELLENMAGNUM: As a streamlined swimmer from ice shelf to ice shelf, your thinking is both efficient and refined, struggling to maintain a straight path unmarked yet remarkably outlined.

T.S. ELIOT: You both have been able to navigate along the earth's magnetic lines, honing your ability to find sustenance in these "bear-en" times.

ANTONIN ARTAUD: To find strength in the face of adversity, swimming through these emotional waters, communicating with the Spirit, through dreams, transformation, becoming a shaman, a mystic and finally, a visionary.

TELLENMAGNUM: Universal energy flows when fear is absent as silence grows.

Lord Byron returned after having disappeared mysteriously, leaving his bear in Tellenmagnum's hands.

LORD BYRON: Though I have never been referred to as "nice man," I can with confidence call you the "Ice Man." Whatever emotion is frozen and blocked, you are there to get it unlocked.

T.S. ELIOT: To keep things from going South, we are all aligned with our Polar North.

TELLENMAGNUM: You talking to me or Lord Byron?

Byron has been smoking opium, helping to contribute to more delirium.

LORD BYRON: Well, both, I guess. Did you know I invited Shelley, his wife, Mary, and Keats without running it by you.

T.S. ELIOT: That's not a problem as long as you told them the ground rules.

98

LORD BYRON: I did, let's see if they remembered. My mind is still in a haze at the moment. I am always ripe for the pipe. You know I was exiled for proliferating accusations of cruelty, adultery and incest with my half-sister. I am back here illegally and have my trustworthy bear as my security.

T.S. ELIOT: You know that this party is also a safe house. You are untouchable while here. The word is that you have always followed you imagination, indulged in your passions and abandoned your children. You have been labeled as mad, bad and dangerous to know.

There is some audible coughing near the door as it is slowly nudged open. The sad face of John Keats is swallowed up by the door frame and the dark night behind.

ERIK SATIE: Keats! So happy that Byron remembered to invite you. Who did you bring?

JOHN KEATS: My sadness. All that is left.

T.S. ELIOT: Shelley called you "a pale flower." Did you happen to run into him along the way.

JOHN KEATS: No but I had to run for my life not too far from here. Some apparition or a kind of monster was after me and I wanted to alert you that it could be still around.

T.S. ELIOT: Tellenmagnum! Did you get that? We may need your services soon.

TELLENMAGNUM: Yes, I am here. The bear and I can handle anything.

Hemingway, crazily, is still carrying the unloaded shotgun in his hands as he now heads back to the bar for another drink.

JOE: What about some water? Look at how high Henry Miller gets purely on this crystalline filler!

Hemingway maintains his back to Henry Miller.

ERNEST HEMINGWAY: Another! Miller! Don't talk to me about him. Never even met the guy. I was already in Paris long before he arrived.

Eliot comes over to the bar to speak to Hemingway.

T.S. ELIOT: Let me keep the gun for you in my study there along with the rest.

Hemingway starts to protest, but then relents and releases the weapon.

T.S. ELIOT: I understand! My nerves are "shot" too. I am just back from a restful cure in Lausanne, when Satie came to me with the idea for this "get together" to help cheer me up.

Socrates strolls by as comfortably as if he still were in the streets of Athens.

SOCRATES: *(Overhearing Eliot)* Plato called this a "Symposium."

T.S. ELIOT: I am scheduled to do a reading coming up in Paris at Silvia Beach's bookstore, "Shakespeare and Co."

ERNEST HEMINGWAY: The "Waste Land?"

T.S. ELIOT: Yes, do you know it?

Hemingway now turns away from Eliot, obviously distracted with his own self-indulging musings.

ERNEST HEMINGWAY: The Paris Years! That was a "fertile wasteland!"

SOCRATES: Would you call this a classroom or a room of class?

Mary Shelley is suddenly upon them as no one saw her slip inside.

LORD BYRON: Mary! You made it! And Percy, your husband, didn't you bring him?

MARY SHELLEY: No, he insisted on going sailing even with a bad storm brewing.

MARY SHELLEY: I brought something else.

LORD BYRON: Something? Not someone?

MARY SHELLEY: It was a story that turned gory. I should not have tried to play God. It's a cautionary tale that helped turn our poet Keats pale. I had to put my overall depression after all those miscarriages into coherent thought.

The main door gets literally smashed down as her "creation" plows into the mansion.

ERNEST HEMINGWAY: Frankenstein! Where is my shotgun!

JOE: Won't help here, macho man. This is no big game to kill, but the ultimate game of will.

LORD BYRON: Your creation, Mary, is upon us in all its futuristic glory.

FRANKENSTEIN: I am not like you think. I am here only in search of a heart. I am all brain and do not want to live out a life in vain.

Mary fumbles inside her bag to clutch what she had brought to the "party." Her small tragic hands clasped its oval shape. What she did not have the courage to tell Byron was that her husband had been taken by the storm and drowned. After his cremation, his heart refused to burn, and she kept the unscathed organ in a silken shroud to carry with her.

MARY SHELLEY: It must be this that Frankenstein knew I had and is after. Since I created him or it—it knows all about me.

FRANKENSTEIN: I need only a heart to cease to be heartless. It is the only way for all of us to survive. Otherwise, I am programmed to maim and kill all in my path.

Mary springs into action and lunges for Frankenstein, ripping out her dead husband's heart for all to see.

MARY SHELLEY: Take it. My husband, Percy, will then live on inside my own literary creation and you will do no more evil.

Frankenstein grabs it greedily and quickly opens his metal chest to hide the most sought-after treasure. Tellenmagnum and the bear both stare in both relief and utter disbelief.

T.S. ELIOT: Suddenly, just like that, a poet's heart saved us all from imminent danger and destruction at the robotic hands of this Frankenstein creature.

Ezra Pound arrives, and almost gets run over by Frankenstein making his quick exit at Eliot's mansion, heading for the surrounding woods.

EZRA POUND: Am I too late for the "festivities?" And who was that monster of a "man" nearly knocking me over on his way out?

T.S. ELIOT: No Ezra, but you did miss the "bears."

EZRA POUND: Bears? And what was that? No bear!

MARY SHELLEY: Its all the fault of my unbridled imagination. An example of my romantic mind over-reaching and breaching boundaries between the human and non-human.

T.S. ELIOT: By the way, thanks for your help on my revision.

EZRA POUND: The artist is always beginning. Any work of art which is not a beginning, an invention or discovery is of little worth.

T.S. ELIOT: Then you came to the right place. We are all here for invention, a beginning and discovery, though there is nothing here that is a convention.

"Out of the blue," we hear from the "cloud" as if it is our constant Greek refrain.

ARISTOPHANES: I am a one-man chorus--to try and connect them to us.

EZRA POUND: Where is that voice coming from?

SOCRATES: My cloudy thoughts you hear--when I am up in the air, I express what I most fear.

Aristophanes now laughs again almost hysterically as Dostoevsky continues writing on the wall with equal intensity unveiling a new mystery. Pound shifts his eyes over to Buster Keaton and looks fixedly at him.

EZRA POUND: Glance is the enemy of vision.

Dostoevsky continues writing and now spouts out freely:

FYODOR DOSTOEVSKY: If you want to overcome the whole world, overcome yourself.

Keaton shifts his focus to Dostoevsky who is completely absorbed with his wall writing much to the chagrin of Dickens and his obsessions with tidiness.

T.S. ELIOT: This party has always been my masterplan to help me recover after the publication of the "Waste Land."

FYODOR DOSTOEVSKY: God is necessary, and therefore must exist...but I know he does not and cannot exist...Don't you understand that a man with these two diverse thoughts cannot go on living?

Chief Bromden, who had accompanied Ken Kesey to Eliot's mansion has said absolutely nothing until this moment. The broom in his hands has nothing to do with Keaton the "mop" nor Dickens and his cleaning fixation.

CHIEF BROMDEN: When I breathed, my breath was lightning. Suddenly the fog starts to move.

The storm had gone on outside unabated. Now we hear another crash of thunder.

HERACLITUS: What did I tell you!

CHIEF BROMDEN: Sometimes dreams are wiser than waking.

SOCRATES: Who is truly awake here?

ARISTOPHANES: *(Still from the cloud)* I am!

Tellenmagnum sees the Big Chief Bromden, who is at least as imposing as he is, and is impressed. He hands the polar bear off to his caretaker, Lord Byron, for the moment, and heads over to the Chief. The storm outside, now for the moment, slows a bit and a night of dense fog starts to roll into the yard and up to the mansion where the door is still wide open.

TELLENMAGNUM: You remind me of a king becoming the mountain it just conquered after a steep ascent.

CHIEF BROMDEN: I am not just a character from a book written by a scribe, but a former chief now with no real tribe.

TELLENMAGNUM: Even through the fog, I can tell you are as strong as a tree, not a fallen log. Your white hospital smock does not pose for me any kind of a shock.

CHIEF BROMDEN: Good, I was hoping you would stand your ground where I once stood, long before there was anything out there I understood.

TELLENMAGNUM: Don't worry about those who deal in what is not real.

CHIEF BROMDEN: If you are coming with me, then, let's go!

T.S. ELIOT: Hey, Chief, what's going on here?

CHIEF BROMDEN: Fighting our way through this fog, we are not part of this huge machinery as a mere cog. That is my takeaway from our "Frankenstein Moment."

Tellenmagnum takes the Chief outside the mansion to the yard and points up in the sky toward the constellation of Ursa Major. Lord Byron and his bear are already out there.

TELLENMAGNUM: That is what I was able to paint on the wall inside the stable. You become what you create which you call destiny or even fate.

The polar bear up on his hind legs appears to be growling at the night sky.

106

CHIEF BROMDEN: It's surprising we can see it through all this night fog.

Back inside the mansion, Grotowski has been observing Buster Keaton for a while and remembers his physicality when the "bears" tossed him back and forth. Buster is now seen running around in a circle as apparently someone or something is chasing him, but we don't know what or who. Dali has gone back to standing on his head seeking more inspiration. Artaud has suddenly removed all his clothes and runs past the bear and Tellenmagnum to disappear in the surrounding wooded area.

JERZY GROTOWSKI: Our scene is now set. We are all involved in our respective roles, and I have chosen my "actor-saint." *(He points to Keaton still running in circles.)* Exhaustion helps to access your emotions more readily as they become more heightened and raw.

Ben Franklin returns to the main hallway to see Grotowski and the others both inside and outside the mansion.

BEN FRANKLIN: I definitely feel an electric current that was not here before. This atmosphere is supercharged! A long life may not be good enough, but a good life is long enough.

Out of that dense fog where Artaud just now disappeared, appears a strange looking man with a white Russian Cossacks cap and long white fur coat. It is none other than the legendary and long-awaited George Gurdjieff.

GEORGE GURDJIEFF: What I possess is impossible for you to carry, but once you have it, it's the lightest thing in the world.

T.S. ELIOT: So, it appears you finally got that message we sent out to you via courier?

GEORGE GURDJIEFF: I finally got it through a dancer in Turkey.

ERIK SATIE: Turkey? Land of the Dervishes!?

GEORGE GURDJIEFF: Whirling Dervishes?

ERIK SATIE: Yes, the very ones. Through the right motion produces enlightened emotion.

Hemingway ambles with difficulty out to see this "Gurdjieff character."

ERNEST HEMINGWAY: You mean you can heal my mood with the right movement?

JERZY GROTOWSKI: Maybe. It's been done before.

GEORGE GURDJIEFF: The question is and has always been--what kind of exercises or movement--no struggle, no progress and no result.

JERZY GROTOWSKI: Break the habit and you lose the "habit."

ERNEST HEMINGWAY: Of the monk!

JERZY GROTOWSKI: Yes, in a way or gain a "way."

Grotowski glances over at his freshly poured drink.

JERZY GROTOWSKI: I imagine your struggle to write will last as long as your body is caught in the web of its past.

EZRA POUND: Move or be moved.

JERZY GROTOWSKI: Or removed.

GEORGE GURDJIEFF: Don't sleep if you want to go deep.

Eliot is looking out into the yard and up into the night sky.

T.S. ELIOT: This storm won't last forever.

Beethoven is also out there in the yard with his white coat flapping in the night wind.

LUDWIG VAN BEETHOVEN: In me it will--I guarantee!

Dali has finally gotten down from his last headstand he had been doing.

SALVADOR DALI: We ARE the mystery.

Aristophanes laughs loudly from his protective cloud.

ARISTOPHANES: That is why I stay hidden up here. It is more than enough to have to hear myself.

ERIK SATIE: I had asked everything to be white for us to contrast the dark stark night.

Satie goes outside and gazes up at the stars. Chief Bromden joins him as he looks up at the "Big Dipper" inside of "Ursa Major."

CHIEF BROMDEN: This is our moment. Let's fill the "Big Dipper" inside of us.

The Chief points to the polar bear who growls contently.

TELLENMAGNUM: All of us possess that "Big Dipper" inside. That is our message from a 30,000-year-old sage.

Pythagoras returns to the conversation.

PYTHAGORAS: I play the lyre to cure the illness of both body and soul. *(He strums on the lyre.)* According to the Harmony of the Spheres, the heavenly bodies move following a mathematical equation which corresponds to musical notes that form part of the Grand Cosmic Creation.

HERACLITUS: True and an unapparent harmony is stronger than an apparent one.

From that same cloud Aristophanes continues with his constant laughter. Then he turns to direct his attention to Socrates.

ARISTOPHANES: I am aware that you alert us to beware of the barrenness of a busy life lived without care. For once we actually agree as you can see up here in my cloud, I am completely idle and free.

SOCRATES: Your "vision" is always cloudy and nebulous, which fits you as you are not naturally credulous.

Aristophanes howls again with laughter as Socrates walks away ignoring his antics.

ARISTOPHANES: You took all those original "round human beings" seriously? Remember my legend? Ha, ha, ha, ha.

SOCRATES: Then, you were joking to my student Plato?

ARISTOPHANES: Always! He was too serious anyway about his Academy, which I never attended by the way. I did, however, like the part about the divided halves in search of their other to complete their previous androgynous selves.

Dali's head is now cleared again, and he blurts out to no one in particular or anyone who cares to listen.

SALVADOR DALI: Compared to the Spanish painter, Velazquez, I am nothing, but compared to contemporary painters, I am the most "big genius" of the modern time.

Dali fingers his white necklace of imitation pearls as George Sand returns to the main hall.

GEORGE SAND: My dear Dali, your demeanor has the slickness of an Argentine tango dancer.

Gala appears for the first time in the doorway as Dali immediately races up to her and throws himself down on his knees.

SALVADOR DALI: Without you my dear Gala, Divine Dali would be insane even with the advantage of having a totally brilliant brain.

Freud strolls nearby to witness the couple engaged.

SIGMUND FREUD: Staircases, keys, dripping candles, melting clocks--you have got all my subconscious symbols right there in paint that shocks.

Chief Bromden still gazes up at the sky through the night blanket of fog as a low clap of thunder resounds.

CHIEF BROMDEN: The sound of thunder means the return of the Thunder Bird--those "thunder beings." You are wondering does the thunder bring the birds of do the birds bring the thunder?

TELLENMAGNUM: Come to know that is the way to grow.

CHIEF BROMDEN: The knower and the known are changed inside, where on the outside its not shown.

TELLENMAGNUM: My painting of Ursa Major didn't represent that constellation, but WAS that constellation in the imagination!

CHIEF BROMDEN: It is as different as the "noun" is from the "verb." Description versus action.

TELLENMAGNUM: When "I" painted that constellation--we became its reality with that "feeling of one created nation.

SALVADOR DALI: What I painted also painted me! I get it! Surrealism made me as much as I made it.

TELLENMAGNUM: Songs sing, healing heals and...

The polar bear growls.

TELLENMAGNUM: ...the growling growls.

Socrates loves this and appears fully committed.

SOCRATES: My method changed me so that they had to...

ARISTOPHANES: ...kill you. *(He laughs so loud it becomes a howl.)* But they...

SOCRATES: Could not kill the "will," which is why I am here--still.

Freud blows a plume of white smoke from his pipe.

SIGMUND FREUD: When we recollect our dreams, we project an infinite playground of a mind unbound.

TELLENMAGNUM: The "Big Dipper" inside our "Ursa Major Bear Cave" contains that "gap" the mind uses to tap.

Direct again from the cloud...

ARISTOPHANES: I constantly refill that "Dipper" when my "cloud bursts."

TELLENMAGNUM: My long hibernation turned out to be 30,000 years of constant meditation.

Einstein returns to the main drawing room to join in on the discussion.

ALBERT EINSTEIN: To get the "Big Dipper" to become a life-changing "tipper," become a quantum "stripper."

Lord Byron has already stripped naked, needing no encouragement and bolts across the yard with his polar bear looking on with curiosity and catching Einstein off guard.

ALBERT EINSTEIN: *(Smiling)* Lord Byron never disappoints.

Freud looks over at Einstein, thoroughly enjoying the plot twists of this new show.

SIGMUND FREUD: Yes, the stripping away of psychological levels. Though I am clearly not sure how picking up cigarette butts off the street to augment your pipe tobacco helped you solve relativity. Sounds like a pipe dream. *(He laughs.)*

ALBERT EINSTEIN: It was my active sex life that improved my cognitive function and promoted neurogenesis, the production of new neurons.

Ben Franklin returns to the mansion, still wet and drying himself. He is walking with "flippers," which he, himself, originally had invented.

BEN FRANKLIN: Just as my daily swim in the chilly Thames did, bathing my brain and vital organs with a flood of fresh flowing blood.

PYTHAGORAS: My 40-day water-only fast boosted mental perception and creativity fast by giving the brain an endorphin release and a well- being blast. Is that what you are talking about?

Tellenmagnum goes over to his friend, the polar bear, who appears to be already missing Lord Byron after he disappeared in the trees.

TELLENMAGNUM: My hibernation was also a stage of incubation. That detachment and mindless wandering allowed all my

114

prehistoric knowledge to marinate and then freeze during the glacial period, leading up to my "cave-awakening."

Mozart suddenly bursts in, bounding across the drawing room, literally jumping from the furniture to the floor and back. Though he had clearly been invited no one thought he would actually show up, least of all Satie.

ERIK SATIE: You are one of my models of what occurs in between the notes.

WOLFGANG AMADEUS MOZART: Yes, Erik, I created complex structures to help order my mind's melodic and harmonic pictures.

Edison is also back, ready to turn on things.

THOMAS EDISON: After 11,000 experiments of learning how to fail, the light finally went on when I refused to bail.

The lights flicker on and off provoked by the electrical storm. Beethoven, outside, looks up at the "Ursa Major Constellation" and the "Big Dipper" shaking his fist.

LUDWIG VAN BEETHOVEN: During my dark night of the soul, I was initiated into the world of silence, and slowly made my way out of this plane of violence.

Heraclitus stands by in silence.

HERACLITUS: The way up and the way down both don the same "gown."

With snow flurries outside in a turbulence of white swirls, Richard Wagner arrives in his all-white polar fur coat.

RICHARD WAGNER: I am here, having survived the wind and rain and now ready to begin my reign.

Nietzsche is back and obviously struggling to feel even-keel.

FRIEDRICH NIETZSCHE: *(To Wagner) I am seeking the cheerful, profound, unique, wanton, tender, roguish and above all-- graceful! You provide me with no pleasing rhythm or melody and give me mere posing and gesturing--more acting than real composing.*

Aristophanes reaches a hand down from the cloud with a cup of Hemlock for Socrates.

ARISTOPHANES: Drink down this cup of hemlock and cure yourself of this endless questioning of life you continually mock.

Socrates reaches for it naturally, unlike before, when as a citizen of Athens was given no other honorable recourse. The storm outside intensifies, causing Wagner's furs to flap more in the wind. That Cloud of Aristophanes has one final burst and he, himself, descends in a downpour on top of the dying Socrates. Scarlatti immediately heads over to the harpsichord and plays furiously and fast.

HERACLITUS: "Amor Fati!" Love your fate! It is too late now for hate.

FRIEDRICH NIETZSCHE: Follow Tellenmagnum and his bear friend. Follow Chief Bromden out of hibernation from his own cave den. Make haste to appreciate cheerfully art's fresh taste.

ERNEST HEMINGWAY: Hey, my refill!?

In through the wide-open front door comes Lord Byron still naked as Eliot quickly throws a white shawl over him as they both stand over Socrates who is slowly dying but still hangs on.

LORD BYRON: I will never drink from that cup formed from a human skull again. No more hanging out with Albanian warlords, but I will still keep my bear. By the way, where is he?

Socrates looks up at Aristophanes to make a plea pointing to Lord Byron.

SOCRATES: Help out this youth!

ARISTOPHANES: Will do what I can.

LORD BYRON: It is too late to reform. All those countless actresses, opera singers, countesses and choirboys. All my works are regarded as blasphemies, making me the most notorious poet in all Europe. It is time to leave again. Tellenmagnum can keep my bear. I will leave now to help the Turks in their fight for independence, but first we have to regroup the Greek fleet.

Demosthenes arrives as Socrates breathes his last breath.

ARISTOPHANES: Impeccable timing Demosthenes, just in time for a speech.

DEMOSTHENES: Eloquence is a great art, but I have also learned when to stop, even before I start.

HERACLITUS: I know you are a man who has had some pretty intimidating roadblocks to overcome.

DEMOSTHENES: You, Aristophanes, always laughed at me in the beginning before I came into my own as an orator.

ARISTOPHANES: You had a certain weakness of voice and indistinctness of speech and shortness of breath, which disturbed the sense of what you said by disjoining your sentences.

DEMOSTHENES: I overcame my impediment with measures like practicing speaking with my mouth full of pebbles.

ARISTOPHANES: I also heard you built an underground study where you could work on your voice for two to three months at a time.

DEMOSTHENES: During that time, I shaved off half my head of hair, to fight off temptation to hang around, and do other things elsewhere.

HERACLITUS: And that ridiculous hairdo had the effect of making you too embarrassed to show yourself in public, thus forcing you to remain in your subterranean chamber to continue your regimen.

The rain continues on along with the howling wind as James Joyce makes his belated appearance.

T.S. ELIOT: Joyce! At last, you have come to join our humble cast. And you are wearing your all-white writing coat.

Joyce holds up his large blue pencil for Eliot to see.

JAMES JOYCE: This is what I use instead of a typewriter. I have been hard at work all day.

T.S. ELIOT: And written...

JAMES JOYCE: Two sentences. I have the words already--what I am seeking is a perfect word order.

HERACLITUS: I get it! You favor quality of writing over speed.

JAMES JOYCE: After numerous failed operations to repair both my eyes, I am nearly blind, caused by inflammation of the iris.

T.S. ELIOT: Still working on "Finnegan's Wake" to make it less indecipherable?

JAMES JOYCE: I am trying to "see" my way through.

T.S. ELIOT: I think Demosthenes, and someone else I know of, who has you beat on ways to overcome distractions. He should be arriving soon.

ERIK SATIE: Who do you mean? Hugo? Victor Hugo?

T.S. ELIOT: Yes, like Lord Byron, he is known for shedding his clothes too.

At that very moment, Hugo bursts in wearing a large thick white shawl with nothing underneath.

VICTOR HUGO: Just finished "Hunchback" and made my deadline!

ERIK SATIE: We heard you had locked away all your formal wear and ordered the servants not to give you any clothes until you had finished the novel.

VICTOR HUGO: Stripped down, I finished it all in a white shawl gown.

ERIK SATIE: Some say you wrote while naked locked up in that room!

VICTOR HUGO: Who will ever know, but the book is there after all of my efforts to show. If you ask: virtue has a veil, vice, a mask.

Dali returns to see Victor Hugo. Dali's hair is long with sideburns, wearing a white stocking cap and gray striped knee breeches. Dali takes out his jewel-studded cigarette case and offers Hugo a mustache, which he had kept inside that case.

SALVADOR DALI: Go ahead Victor, take one! They are "sacred," my personal business card!

VICTOR HUGO: I heard you ring your bell and came to hear what you had to tell.

SALVADOR DALI: Your amazing artwork foreshadows what we did as Surrealists!

Dali's white cape blows from the wind coming in through the door. He raises up his "white" walking stick.

SALVADOR DALI: I am blind to my conscious mind!

VICTOR HUGO: Which painters do you admire most?

SALVADOR DALI: First Dali, after that there are no others. Oh, wait, as I said before, first Velazquez!

Wagner is back hearing Dali's voice. He returns with his favorite dog, a King Charles Spaniel named "Pep." He is talking to "Pep" as they move forward towards the harpsichord.

RICHARD WAGNER: Listen to this, Pep!

He plays a short melody in E-flat major. Pep goes completely quiet, calmly waging his tail. Then Pep gets up on his hind legs in excitement as Wagner continues on playing that melody. Dali, quietly observing the show, starts to laugh.

SALVADOR DALI: Does he also give you correctional tips on how to better compose?

RICHARD WAGNER: You a mind reader? Of course! "Pep" has his own stool next to mine and helps me out when I play like a fool.

Dali whirls his white cape, slams down his walking stick in deep laughter.

RICHARD WAGNER: During the writing of "Tannhauser" and "Lohengrin," when I had trouble with a passage, I would turn to "Pep" for his reaction and rewrite the piece according to his direction.

SALVADOR DALI: And they say I am the surreal, crazy one!

Who knows where Schiller had run off to, but he comes back hearing Beethoven walking around singing notes to his "Ode to Joy" theme for his Ninth Symphony. Schiller had just taken a strong inhale of some rotting apples he was still carrying around in his pocket to clear his head. Beethoven walks right by him without noticing his presence, so engrossed in the humming of his infectious melody. Schiller then heads to the bar and orders.

FRIEDRICH SCHILLER: Don't worry about that strong scent around me. It is of spiced apples which calm me, even lowering my blood pressure.

Beethoven recognizes his friend Schiller and tries very hard to hear what he is saying.

FRIEDRICH SCHILLER: I also have heard that rosemary and lemon in the morning and lavender in the evening can improve cognitive functioning. Lavender helps to keep pain under control. Getting a massage with aromatic oils lowers anxiety and helps ward off depression. I even forgot now what I was drinking. I think the apple scent is working—truly heaven-sent.

LUDWIG VAN BEETHOVEN: Friedrich, my head is pounding with this theme and a dozen other threads of sound. How can I calm it down?

122

FRIEDRICH SCHILLER: Let's find some more aromas of basil, thyme, mint and lilac.

LUDWIG VAN BEETHOVEN: What? Oh! Yes. Lead the way!

Dali is now whirling with the wind and waving his cane as if attempting to direct its "elementals."

SALVADOR DALI: No sane mind can prove its own sanity. Any mind that believes it can prove its own sanity is, therefore, truly insane.

We are back at the death scene of Socrates, who still has not released his last breath..

SOCRATES: I am truly that gadfly, that one who interferes with the status quo of the community by asking novel, potently upsetting, questions, usually directed at authorities.

ARISTOPHANES: Now this fly has been swatted.

SOCRATES: My questions have all been in the service of truth, that sword, to cut down all lies.

Socrates now gasps for air.

ARISTOPHANES: Guilty or not guilty, you have been freed from your prison by drinking the poison.

Socrates gasps one final breath and utters:

SOCRATES: Write one last play and name it: "The Flies!"

Socrates dies as Eliot now picks up the empty poison cup.

T.S. ELIOT: Do you think it was made from a human skull as Lord Byron claimed before he fled for Greece?

ERIK SATIE: It is all now so symbolic. It is our own head or heads that contain their own magic to save and to think, not to empty its poison to drink.

Heraclitus returns to this scene of the crime hearing another clap of thunder.

HERACLITUS: That sound is pure power unbound. We are struck by lightning that for an open mind is not frightening.

Tellenmagnum holds up his huge cave painting brush one more time.

TELLENMAGNUM: Red Ochre is our color treasure to paint all the world for pleasure. Its birth tone comes from the earth.

Lord Byron's bear stares intently into the face of Tellenmagnum as if he truly understood. Pep, the spaniel, leaves Wagner's side and goes over to the bear, sits and raises his paw.

SALVADOR DALI: It is through paint that the sword of the brush points to the saint.

VINCENT VAN GOGH: Was it really you who cut off my ear when I turned on you on the way to the bordello?

PAUL GAUGUIN: Are you still in a state of shock?

VINCENT VAN GOGH: Yes! I can reply to you by drawing with my own "sword-brush!"

124

TELLENMAGNUM: Your blood drawn is close to the Red Ochre color of the sun at dawn.

PAUL GAUGUIN: I saw it in Tahiti!

VINCENT VAN GOGH: I prefer "yellow ochre," from the sun of the South.

Charles Dickens strolls in with a copy of his new journal: "All the Year Round."

CHARLES DICKENS: I just got permission from T.S. To include whomever I choose for this week's publication of my new journal: "All the Year Round."

VINCENT VAN GOGH: Can you include my new color experiments with "yellow ochre?"

CHARLES DICKENS: We are in our opening days of business, but I am here at this "Symposium" or "Convivium" to collect our best ideas for the journal.

T.S. ELIOT: It is our moment to seize this "sword," in order to publish all our ideas based on the creative use of the "word."

ERIK SATIE: Richard, don't look so dismayed, as if you had been ignored; there will be ample room for musical samples of what you have recently scored.

RICHARD WAGNER: Here we can speak out, frankly, take risks, or be prone to hubris--even making speeches that are heartfelt and noble evoking the iris.

T.S. ELIOT: Now that Socrates is gone, there is a void to fill we can no longer avoid.

Aristophanes has completely descended from the "cloud" after the death of Socrates and roams freely among the others at Eliot's Cocktail Party.

ARISTOPHANES: I have vowed to avoid all hard-drinking after drowning myself in it without thinking.

JOE: Good for you.

ARISTOPHANES: After I was told by Socrates in his last words to write, "The Flies" as my next play, I fell into a kind of reverie worrying about how it could see the light of day.

JOE: His last joke for you in jest, was meant to bring out your best.

ARISTOPHANES: Once I begin it, nothing will stop me.

ERIK SATIE: You have a knack for finding beauty and worth in uncommon places, are quick to act and never miss an opportunity--the secret of your ingenuity.

ARISTOPHANES: In a dream last night I saw a fly feasting on something sweet and then later went for meat before I awoke in a cold sweat.

Freud overheard this dream rendition and made his comment.

SIGMUND FREUD: That's all good news Aristophanes! It is both a message of abundance and prosperity that are sure to come. The fly eating the carrion symbolizes your death and rebirth

126

cycles. Something in you has changed and is now dying to be reborn.

The polar pear became Tellenmagnum's constant companion after Lord Byron's flight of fancy. The bear appears to be aware of everything going on. Freud glances over nervously at it eyeing him, not eight feet away. The polar bear slowly pulled itself down out of attack mode to sit. Relieved, Freud continued talking to Aristophanes.

SIGMUND FREUD: Try to sense those flies to feel their buzz. Befriend a grasshopper to put the spring back into all you bring.

ARISTOPHANES: Grasshopper?! Interesting, though my best work might have already been done; I still have the heart for art to have fun.

SIGMUND FREUD: Are you referring to "Lysistrata," where the women denied their men sex and thus, no trip to the stratosphere?

ARISTOPHANES: Now you got me thinking about that play during which I did absolutely nothing but "play." There were lines like this: "So one day, Lysistrata, equipped with all the data reckoned upon, a tactic to withhold love climatic." And then a little later I recall: "She aimed to end all conflict with some cohorts she had picked to flaunt breast and nothing hide till peace could reside, men were denied."

SIGMUND FREUD: To withhold the act of sex —hmmm, interesting tactic.

ARISTOPHANES: Once it started there was no stopping, words literally jumping onto the page as its "main course" along with supplemental topping.

SIGMUND FREUD: And now you are thinking about the ticking clock, or have you come down with a case of "writer's block?"

ARISTOPHANES: None of the above; this one is also about love. Not for the deep blue skies but for a mysterious swarm of flies.

Freud continues listening, riveted and puffing on his cigar as Dickens is also listening nearby.

SIGMUND FREUD: Can't wait!

CHARLES DICKENS: I can publish your first scenes in my magazine: "All the Year Round."

Aristophanes continues musing, now talking to himself.

ARISTOPHANES: None of my flies will know anything. Their incessant buzzing sound will be like the asking of questions all around. Anyone who knows anything will be immediately swarmed, and with questions be sternly warned. The "Soul of Socrates" now flies free.

Nietzsche has been in a state of agitated reflection all this time and can control himself no longer:

FRIEDRICH NIETZSCHE: We are looking for a new ruler of the unseen realm of the air!

Dostoevsky finally turns away from his beloved wall.

FYODOR DOSTOEVSKY: One cannot approach the subject of "the end" lightly. It is one of the most powerful, incredible devices in the universe.

Voltaire roves around in and out of different conversations.

VOLTAIRE: Within the gray matter of our mind are various twists, turns and labyrinths of a directional kind.

Eliot also has his own reality bites to offer.

T.S. ELIOT: The essential advantage for a poet is not to have a beautiful world with which to deal; it is to be able to see beneath both beauty and ugliness, to see the boredom, and the horror, and the glory as the beginning of the story.

He heads over to Joe's bar feeling he deserves a drink.

JOE: You're in charge, what can I get you to make your spirit enlarge?

T.S. ELIOT: I am a gin man and I love martinis--nothing is quite as stimulating as a strong dry martini cocktail.

In the background we hear a strong "meow!"

T.S. ELIOT: Come here "Noilly-Prat!"

JOE: *(Laughs) Best on the rocks and dry, as you like it, I heard.*

FYODOR DOSTOEVSKY: All the months are cruel, not just April. The busily creative hand can ill afford to waste any fertile ground overseen by the lord.

ERNEST HEMINGWAY: *(To Joe)* I have asked you repeatedly to procure the "Green Fairy" for me to be able to finish my most recent story.

JOE: You mean that concoction you once called: "Death in the Afternoon" if I recall correctly?

ERNEST HEMINGWAY: Yes, of course. You remember how to make it, right? Pour a jigger of absinthe into a champagne glass, then add iced champagne until it attains the proper opalescent milkiness.

Marcel Proust, part of Eliot's literary group, arrives to help show "the way back" for all who are present.

MARCEL PROUST: You are all now officially invited to my celebratory dinner, complete with good food and of course many, many drinks.

JOE: What will it be Monsieur Proust? Your usual, Veuve Clicquot?

Joe pours as Proust nods his head and drinks.

MARCEL PROUST: Suddenly I feel happiness penetrating my whole existence. That "Road Back," must go through all my thinking and to even renew my own style of drinking.

Shaw has wandered back by the bar but is not drinking.

GEORGE BERNARD SHAW: The reasonable man adapts himself to the world. The unreasonable one persists in trying to adapt the world to himself. Therefore, all progress depends on the unreasonable man.

JOE: The world is not run by sense but by nonsense--the world of quantum physics!

GEORGE BERNARD SHAW: Making too much sense is nonsense and too little sense is just being insensitive. We are not here to find our self, but to create it.

Franklin had never really left us since his opening "air bath."

BEN FRANKLIN: The road to publishing is long and winding, leading to your own style, which is the most important finding. The road dictates your style which, in turn, influences what you compile.

There is some hubbub again at the front door of the mansion as George Orwell is seen arriving with Muriel, his favorite white goat.

GEORGE ORWELL: It was Muriel who first taught me how to scale mountains; the most notorious was of self-doubt, which I eventually conquered enabling me to enter my "inner fountains."

GEORGE BERNARD SHAW: Both you and Franklin were swimmers, so it must have been a watery road.

GEORGE ORWELL: I channel some of my creative energy into the swimming of the "channel." On the French side, I earned my coffee and croissant before swimming back to my native haunt.

Muriel bleats as goats do and starts to pull on Dostoevsky's pant leg, breaking him away from his "writing on the wall." At this same moment, Eliot needs to rush again to the front door, as guests continue to arrive. He opens it with a start as a 23-foot-long albino boa constrictor slithers in through the door.

T.S. ELIOT: Mary! Is this your second guest? We all thought you had left the party for good.

Mary Shelley picks up her boa and wraps it around her shoulders like a white shawl. She speaks directly to Lord Byron's polar bear.

MARY SHELLEY: Your master taught me how to think faster. I have transcended that Frankenstein apparition I once created. Now I am back for good as long as my boa does not hug me too hard.

Satie now comes around due to the recent commotion and sees Shelley with her boa.

ERIK SATIE: They call me weird with all my obsessions, especially for the color "white." White is my moon that rises during the night and flies high like a kite, right Mr. Franklin?

Franklin hears him but ignores the remark as Satie is still staring at the boa and Shelley. Shelley looks down at her albino boa still wrapped around her like an elegant white shawl.

MARY SHELLEY: I write until my "boa" becomes restless and begins to squeeze, then I stop writing for the day to enjoy the evening breeze.

ERIK SATIE: Your boa constrictor makes your buddy, Byron's Bear, look so tame, and now even less of a claim to fame.

MARY SHELLEY: I know you are impressed with her color, Erik. Though rare in the wild, her albino pigment disorder has nothing to do with what she was fed and is more common in captivity where they are selectively bred.

ERIK SATIE: She looks to be part of your serpentine road back in time that becomes ever more difficult to define.

T.S. ELIOT: A most distinguished and romantic keepsake-- make no mistake.

Beethoven returns to the bar to drink and talk to Joe.

LUDWIG VAN BEETHOVEN: Genius has to be founded on major talent, but it also adds a freshness and wildness of imagination, a raging ambition, an unusual gift for learning and growing in depth and breadth of thought and spirit...

Joe listens and then points to Mary Shelley

JOE: ...And heart--which is where you start! Didn't Thoreau once say: "It is the worshippers of beauty, after all, who have done the real pioneer work of the world!"?

LUDWIG VAN BEETHOVEN: What?! Who?!...Oh...Yes! Beauty! Beauty is now and forever mine--it is the core of our own precious ore--how we create it is who we are!

JOE: More beer?

Beethoven grabs another mug and guzzles it aggressively.

LUDWIG VAN BEETHOVEN: Schopenhauer got it right by saying: "Talent hits a target no one else can get. Genius hits a target no one else can see.

All along, Van Gogh has been struggling to discover his own road back to sanity.

VINCENT VAN GOGH: How many have become desperate in Paris and lost that "Road Back."

ERIK SATIE: I know.

VINCENT VAN GOGH: Every attempt in the direction of success is worthy of respect. One must not begin by despairing; even if one loses here and there, the point is nevertheless to revive and have courage even though things don't turn out as one first thought.

T.S. ELIOT: Is this road we are on leading to gladness, sadness, or madness?

At the door is none other than William Wordsworth, complete with his white quill in his hand, ready to carry out his "will." He enters talking about the supposed madness of William Blake.

WILLIAM WORDSWORTH: There was no doubt this poor man was mad, but there is something in the madness of this man which interests me more than the "sanity" of Lord Byron and Walter Scott.

ERIK SATIE: Where is William Blake, by the way? Working on the white wings of one of his "visionary angels?"

T.S. ELIOT: It is interesting William, how you refer to Lord Byron and his white polar bear as sane.

WILLIAM WORDSWORTH: That's a long subject, Thomas. In a nutshell we don't see art and literature as merely a means of self-improvement or a spur of good news...

T.S. ELIOT: Go on!

WILLIAM WORDSWORTH: We often present moral ambiguity by providing the reader with no comfortable psychological position.

ERIK SATIE: If Blake had come, he would have loved everything, especially Mary Shelley's boa constrictor.

With renewed commotion at Joe's bar, Oscar Wilde has made his appearance, impeccably dressed as a typical dandy, all in white of course. Joe looks to Wilde ready to offer him a drink.

JOE: Mr. Eliot made it clear that I was to provide all of our evening's specials on demand.

OSCAR WILDE: Which were?

JOE: French 75, Sidecar, Beefeater Gin Martini and Ramos Fizz.

OSCAR WILDE: I just assumed you knew mine!

Wilde notices Joe staring at his clothes.

OSCAR WILDE: As I have always said, "one can never be overdressed or overeducated."

JOE: It's not that Mr. Wilde. I was staring to try to remember your drink.

OSCAR WILDE: That one drink that makes you see things as you wish they were: absinthe!

JOE: Ahhhhh---yes, but of course!

OSCAR WILDE: It also helps me really believe what I have always said that life imitates art rather than the other way around.

JOE: Explain!

OSCAR WILDE: We notice London fogs because art and literature taught us to do so.

JOE: You sure dress the part of an impeccably attired and well-mannered dandy figure, whose life in fact has been a work of art.

OSCAR WILDE: You guessed it.

JOE: You, Mr. Wilde, possess that rare art of seeming to be interested in all that I have to say.

OSCAR WILDE: Why not! A monologue man, however clever, cannot be a gentleman at heart. Besides, men only hear men AND bartenders.

JOE: I guess I say "thanks," though not sure if I agree.

136

Hemingway drifts back to the bar but avoids the conversation with Oscar Wilde, who also discretely avoids him. Hemingway now pauses over his mojito.

ERNEST HEMINGWAY: That stoic philosopher, Seneca, once said: "There is nothing noble in being superior to some other man. The true nobility is in being superior to your own previous self.

JOE: He would also say that philosophers inwardly ought to be different in all respects, but their exterior should conform to society.

Hemingway takes a deep swig on that note...

ERNEST HEMINGWAY: Hmmmmm. Didn't he also advocate plain living but not penance. One can be plain and neat at the same time.

Hemingway nods his head in the direction of Wilde.

ERNEST HEMINGWAY: Doubt if he ever read Seneca! *(He laughs.)*

JOE: Didn't he also talk about the household and dishes in particular?

T.S. ELIOT: *(Overhearing)* Yes, a great man uses earthenware dishes as if they were silver; but he equally uses silver as if it were earthenware.

JOE: Don't you both agree that we need all kinds of challenging tasks to spark our interest throughout the day?

Aristophanes suddenly returns carrying a large scroll in his right hand. Then he holds up the fully written scroll to unroll.

ARISTOPHANES: It's done!! The play called: "The Flies," as you all know, inspired by the "Death of Socrates."

JOE: I can already feel the "buzz" in the air.

ARISTOPHANES: In it I show the four main roads that the soul or spirit can follow towards that ever-effervescent goal of happiness!

T.S. ELIOT: Which are?

ARISTOPHANES: I know nothing more than what "flies"--I just listen for the buzz!

T.S. ELIOT: And?

ARISTOPHANES: Those "flies" buzz to me four different tunes: Epicureanism and the Art of Pleasure, Stoicism, Skepticism and doubt, and last and maybe least, Cynicism and defying convention.

JOE: Why am I not surprised?!

ARISTOPHANES: Each swarm of flies embraces each one of these "behavioral norms."

Wilde has now returned with another glass of absinthe in his hand.

OSCAR WILDE: Now I get that whole Socrates "know nothing" routine. He had tried all four of your "ways," Aristophanes, and chose none of them.

ARISTOPHANES: To simplify things let's imagine that annoying "buzz of flies" can only be stopped through our relation to it.

JOE: How so?

ARISTOPHANES: Enjoy their "buzz," accept that buzz as fate, doubt its power or even its existence, and finally defy its presence. "We" determine which of the four is best by seeing each one only in the light of jest.

ERIK SATIE: I am already laughing and can't wait for "The Flies."

Einstein has also circled around to Joe and his bar.

ALBERT EINSTEIN: I feel in a hurry and cramped in here for space.

ERIK SATIE: Wouldn't you call this time and space issue you have all relative?

Einstein laughs out loud as he downs a beer.

HONORÉ DE BALZAC: *(Adding quickly)* Just slow down.

ALBERT EINSTEIN: There is no time! But listening to those four options of Aristophanes as the road back to ourselves, I would have to choose all four--dimensions.

ARISTOPHANES: You calling "The Flies" a "spacetime" vision?

ALBERT EINSTEIN: Yes! Each one defines an extension of each dimension.

ARISTOPHANES: I feel now as though my play has "flown away." And I am, as usual, just left with the "buzz."

Hemingway perks up upon hearing the word "buzz."

ERNEST HEMINGWAY: Why is that such a bad thing?

Aristophanes laughs.

ARISTOPHANES: I believe our dear departed friend, Socrates, would be happy to know that none of his "flying souls" know what their next move will be. Their "light" is to be continually in multidimensional flight.

ALBERT EINSTEIN: I wouldn't be against that plight as my next groundbreaking insight.

ARISTOPHANES: The soul is now defined as a "swarm of insight," as refined as it is so inclined. *(He laughs.)*

Dali now returns with his pet, "Babou," an ocelot on a leash with a diamond-studded collar. He goes right up to where Aristophanes, Eliot and Einstein are conversing.

SALVADOR DALI: I am the foremost painter of light, but I refuse to do anything here in England. It is the most unpleasant place. I must prefer the pain of my beloved and long-lost Spain. Have you met Babou?

Dali proceeds to show off his pet. Eliot shudders throughout this whole experience.

SALVADOR DALI: Thomas, my dear, there is nothing to fear. Babou is just a normal cat I painted over with this "op art" design.

Eliot takes more than a step back, disbelieving all that Dali is saying, as he, Tellenmagnum and "The Bear" approach him.

T.S. ELIOT: *(Thinking to himself)* These two really seem to be hitting it off.

ERIK SATIE: What is that long string attached to, that you hold in your other hand?

SALVADOR DALI: Oh that! To all my paintings I have brought with me. Though I am here to paint "light," I never am able to travel light.

Satie's eyes follow that long string back to a "boatload of paintings." Samuel Beckett is now back on the scene, impressed by Dali and Babou.

SAMUEL BECKETT: Waiting is much more delicious than any kind of whimsical partaking. We are on the road, which is as light as what we carry as our load.

SALVADOR DALI: If you already have "light," then I don't have to paint it anymore.

ERIK SATIE: Though you once painted the "Last Supper," I can see no sign of you doing the "Resurrection!"

Dali, distracted, looks into Babou's eyes.

SALVADOR DALI: I have had to protect myself from my muse, Gala, who had the libido of an electric eel and went after anything and everything that would make her "feel."

T.S. ELIOT: Our passion here is definitely not for money, power and notoriety, but to put art out in front, to ward off ever encroaching anxiety.

SALVADOR DALI: I and my muse, Gala, the demonic dominatrix, are actually as of now out of the mix.

Out of that blue, cold and stormy night, in swirl of fog and wind, appears Hippocrates, the famous Greek physician, credited for allying philosophy and medicine.

HIPPOCRATES: First, I want you all to know that I have not been able to "cure" the madness of Democritus.

ARISTOPHANES: I could have told you that. Whether for sadness or madness, he cannot stop laughing at anything and everything.

HIPPOCRATES: I found that Democritus is not mad but a very wise man whose yearning for solitude and serenity constrains him to discriminate himself from ordinary people by an odd behavior. Deep inside he is melancholic!

ARISTOPHANES: He was called the "Laughing Philosopher" and felt that there were "soul atoms" in the world. I have put him in my new play: "The Flies."

142

Democritus suddenly arrives and appears to be able to speak out for himself. He comes carrying a model of the "atoms" he discovered.

DEMOCRITUS: By desiring little, a poor man makes himself rich.

T.S. ELIOT: This appears to have become "the Night of the Living Greeks."

ARISTOPHANES: Do you have a problem with that Mr. Eliot?

Before he could even respond, Beethoven returns with his usual loud singing and raving while Freud is right there to comment, pointing to Beethoven.

SIGMUND FREUD: There you have a perfect example of the manifestation of the power of the Subconscious Mind when feely allowed to surface.

ARISTOPHANES: If only I could get him to do the music for "The Flies!"

Beethoven plays an "air-piano," as though he had found his widely-spaced triadic chords to play all over the keyboard.

ARISTOPHANES: See what I mean. He is that ideal composer for "The Flies." It's pure "buzz" as if his fingers had taken flight mirroring the "flies'" wing movements to the left and then to the right.

LUDWIG VAN BEETHOVEN: I will not be contained within a suffocating smallness of purpose and will fight on in eternal defense of the Creative Spirit and against all the forces which continually try to corrupt it and contract its ever-noble act.

Fredrich Nietzsche returns specifically to encounter Beethoven, his counterpart in music.

FRIEDRICH NIETZSCHE: I have only a single term for our current populace of so-called philosophers: cabbage-heads! I stand alone among them--that lone sunflower looming high above their rows of all green heads.

LUDWIG VAN BEETHOVEN: Bravo! My play is getting written for me day by day.

FRIEDRICH NIETZSCHE: Difficulties of every sort are welcomed by those of us who are in a continual search.

LUDWIG VAN BEETHOVEN: Fate is knocking just like in my "Fifth."

FRIEDRICH NIETZSCHE: It is "my" fate to have been the first descent human being. I have a terrible fear that I shall one day be pronounced "holy!"

LUDWIG VAN BEETHOVEN: Our very first Philosopher-Saint!

FRIEDRICH NIETZSCHE: It seems to me that to take a book of mine into one's hands is one of the rarest distinctions that anyone can confer upon oneself. I even assume that "he" removes his shoes when he does-- not to speak of boots!

ARISTOPHANES: Wonderful Holy Thinker, if the reader died from the book's impact, they would not have boots on to anchor a disincarnated spirit.

Van Gogh senses the excitement and reappears, still covering his ear, as Beethoven notices his arrival into the drawing room.

VINCENT VAN GOGH: I am still awaiting life's greatest rewards from my constant "brush" with adversity, as you, Friedrich, have claimed.

Beethoven does not hear the dialog even with his ear funnel and now yells out.

LUDWIG VAN BEETHOVEN: Vincent! That you?--Van Gogh?

Van Gogh shows his missing ear and wound to Beethoven.

VINCENT VAN GOGH: You could not tell or just see that I am he?

LUDWIG VAN BEETHOVEN: *(Now even crazier)* You have destroyed half of what I so desperately need to be employed.

Nietzsche is ignoring their interplay and spouts out.

FRIEDRICH NIETZSCHE: To those human beings who are of any concern to me, I wish suffering, desolation, sickness, ill-treatment, indignation--I wish that they should not remain unfamiliar with profound self-contempt, the torture of self-mistrust, the wretchedness of the vanquished. I have no pity for them, because it is with them that the only thing that they can prove today is whether one is worth anything or not— that one endures.

In this brief interim, Van Gogh miraculously gets his cut off ear returned to him.

VINCENT VAN GOGH: My lost ear is now back with me, here. Returned by that woman I had sent it to for being refused and spurned.

Both Democritus and Aristophanes now howl with laughter at this pathetic pair.

ARISTOPHANES: It seems as though the "ears" have it...or do they?

T.S. ELIOT: Excuse me Mr. "Playwright," but the "I's" have it you mean to say.

ARISTOPHANES: Eyes or ears—it's all the same, let's "face" it! Don't get too sensitive on me now, Thomas.

Lou-Andreas Salome enters the party unannounced, taking Satie by surprise. She is wearing a white sheep's skin to keep warm.

LOU ANDREAS SALOME: I heard that both Freud and Nietzsche were here, but to be honest I was looking for Rilke.

ERIK SATIE: You are drenched!

LOU ANDREAS SALOME: I stepped into a cloudburst on the way here.

ARISTOPHANES: Did I hear the word "cloud?" That is something I can speak of out loud.

ERIK SATIE: You mean Rainier Maria Rilke?

LOU ANDREAS SALOME: Is there any other? His diffidence and determination made him irresistible to me.

Now Freud rushes in with a fever to see Salome, his old friend.

SIGMUND FREUD: You are the only one I know who has probed deep into the human psyche.

LOU ANDREAS SALOME: Something deep inside, hot with sheer life, rejoiced and was ever bent on getting out.

SIGMUND FREUD: I never knew how to deal with your emancipation--you are far ahead of your time.

FRIEDRICH NIETZSCHE: After you, Lou, Zarathustra first spoke to me.

ARISTOPHANES: Maybe I am wasting my time writing this new play, "The Flies!"

Nietzsche is shouting out to the clouds themselves.

FRIEDRICH NIETZSCHE: From which stars did we fall to meet each other here?

ARISTOPHANES: Stars? I knew my head was in the clouds but...

FRIEDRICH NIETZSCHE: I am referring to Ms. Salome over there, embroiled with Freud. She always pictures me as a religious genius confronted with the death of God.

ARISTOPHANES: Then we will resurrect him...or her...or the two as in my myth.

FRIEDRICH NIETZSCHE: Yes, that is, I recall, where the two once severed souls reunite to culminate it all.

ARISTOPHANES: My happy ending for "The Flies!"

Salome removes her white sheep's skin.

ARISTOPHANES: You look as lovely and as transparent as a serene cirrus cloud.

FRIEDRICH NIETZSCHE: You were right. My god, Dionysus, died a violent death but was brought to life again, and his sufferings, death and resurrection have always been enacted in sacred rites.

ARISTOPHANES: You must be reading my mind.

FRIEDRICH NIETZSCHE: How so?

ARISTOPHANES: It is all in my new play. He is a traveling teacher much like Socrates and performed miracles of the mind. He was called the "god of wine," since he turned water into it.

Thunder booms and lightning cracks from the storm, still raging with great force. Then, the last thing one would expect happens! Socrates reappears, mounted on an ass, resurrected and coming through the door, which the wind has now flung open wide.

SHAKESPEARE: *(Seeing the apparition)* But love is blind, and lovers cannot see. What am I now seeing?

ARISTOPHANES: Well done Mr. Eliot. You are much more than a banker or the writer of "Wasteland." You are the "maker of myths," as you have done here.

ERIK SATIE: Yes, what a shock. Your Dionysus is no other than our controversial philosopher, Socrates, back from the dead.

ARISTOPHANES: Who mixed that hemlock, anyway?

He quickly glances over at Joe, the bartender.

JOE: Don't look at me. I don't go beyond absinthe for our friend, Oscar Wilde, that dandy wild man.

SOCRATES: Though I have donned this white panther's skin to protect me from the cold, I am definitely not that vine-crowned Dionysus of old.

ARISTOPHANES: This is not how "The Flies" was supposed to fly.

SOCRATES: You know I am not who and how you "painted" me to be. I have come from the front lines and once charged for shielding Alcibiades from the piercing blows of lance and spear.

Hippocrates now has unexpectedly returned.

HIPPOCRATES: Yes Socrates, I know how you, as warrior sophist, fought like a tethered lion unwilling to leave your wounded friend until the Athenian pushed the line forward to envelope their comrades in safety.

SOCRATES: Aristophanes! Were you in on this ploy?

ARISTOPHANES: I was the one who diluted it at the bartender's request so that you could after three days safely return to our party nest.

SIGMUND FREUD: I can't help but see that you have mounted the "ass" of your own ego.

SHAKESPEARE: My "Bottom" is now on top!

ARISTOPHANES: You are trying to convince us that you really wrote "Midsummer's Night Dream." Dream on William. It would take more than "Puck" to accomplish that.

LOU ANDREAS SALOME: The "bottom-line" is that Socrates is back.

ARISTOPHANES: And you, Shakespeare, are the ass, not Bottom, who merely wears the head.

T.S. ELIOT: Can't we all just get along?

SOCRATES: I am the one who mingles freely among Sophists and Warriors alike. Physical exploits of thinkers have been under appreciated just as philosophical exploits of great warriors have been overlooked.

JOE: *(Shouting out)* Drinks are now on the house! Let's drink to this new Man! I have seen it all here from behind my bar as I have not been barred. Being not a drinker, nor professional thinker, makes me free to tinker.

Joe serves up Hemingway one more mojito as he has returned to be first in line at the bar followed by Fitzgerald.

JOE: Education in classical civilization was designed to create the optimal balanced man.

SIGMUND FREUD: Balanced?! Never seen one!

JOE: The warrior gifted in sword play was encouraged to paint, to write, and to play an instrument to connect to the Spirit, and to study math and sciences.

SOCRATES: This is my new question.

ARISTOPHANES: Which is?

SOCRATES: Where does the path of many paths lead?

FRIEDRICH NIETZSCHE: A Renaissance! The complete Man and Woman.

ARISTOPHANES: United together at last!

Dali returns with his "Last Supper" painting draped around him like a cape.

SALVADOR DALI: I heard the word "resurrection" being spoken and wanted to offer my services as a sample "savior" token.

ERIK SATIE: As an accomplished musical illiterate, or so I have been told, I cannot pass judgement on such a painting so bold.

T.S. ELIOT: Socrates has been resurrected, not for being our "savior," but for the astuteness of his inquisitive behavior.

SALVADOR DALI: I have not managed to even save myself, which therefore qualifies me to attempt to save others!

JOE: Though I don't drink, I'll drink to that in the strictest of surrealist tradition. Absinthe anyone?

ARISTOPHANES: How time flies! My play spreads its own tiny wings while, praise be, who has grown sings.

SOCRATES: Slowly your face appears from out of the mist as I have taken another look just to get your gist.

ARISTOPHANES: I am ready now to reascend to my "cloud-of-memory," to finish the rest of "The Flies'" story.

Freud returns with Salome as Aristophanes looks on.

ARISTOPHANES: Soon we will be treated with two "shrinks" for the price of one if the ego has, in fact, retreated.

LOU ANDREAS SALOME: If I dance, it is not for your head on a platter to be able to choose silence over chatter.

SIGMUND FREUD: Your wish for Aristophanes to return to the cloud can now be fulfilled, just as you, Aristophanes, secretly wished for Socrates to be resurrected.

SHAKESPEARE: Like "The Flies" swarm, ideas bombard my mind leaving it less cool than warm. There is much ado about nothing which is always something.

ARISTOPHANES: That main character of your life that you created called "Shakespeare" does not judge. How is it that you do not grow defensive or dismissive when you encounter something that challenges your own principles?

SHAKESPEARE: That need for continuity is one of the greatest challenges that you face as you create your own creed.

SIGMUND FREUD: It seems you have that ability to understand human thought from the inside where your characters fought.

T.S. ELIOT: Human beings have the habit of making a decision based more on their intuitions and emotions than on cognitive reasoning with logical precision.

ARISTOPHANES: Reasoning or seasoning? That is the question, right Mr. Shakespeare?

SHAKESPEARE: The human mind is simply too weak to have a clear and perfect vision of reality, in its ever-changing, ever-moving totality.

Aristophanes now drifts back up to his cloud, where he will reside from now on, as Socrates has fully returned and resurrected.

ARISTOPHANES: I will be able to finish "The Flies" here in the cloud where this swarm of ideas is stored and will also by my ascended spirit's shroud.

ERIK SATIE: All this obsession I have for "white" is to prepare the mind for the uninvestigated sight of insight.

SHAKESPEARE: Gracefully transitioning from one idea to another leaves us open to the most absurd combination of elements we must not smother.

ARISTOPHANES: Up here in my ethereal atmosphere, I am swimming in this seething cauldron of the "now," yet where is "here?"

SHAKESPEARE: I know well that state of bewildering activity where everything is either fizzling or bubbling between what is and is not finite.

ARISTOPHANES: Now, again hidden from that light I can see all that is down there in plain sight.

Socrates comes back into the visual field of Aristophanes.

SOCRATES: I see that it behooves me to loosen up and move outside the grooves. Just because I am on track does not mean that someone has got my back.

ARISTOPHANES: I am writing "The Flies" in longhand as a counterbalance to my mind that always thinks in shorthand.

SHAKESPEARE: Pay close attention to the relationship between the story and the characters in terms of verbs of action...

ARISTOPHANES: Rather than in nouns that tend to separate things out...?

SHAKESPEARE: Action rather than fraction or faction.

SOCRATES: After my "resurrection," there is no more method. Since my mind is now prepared for...

ARISTOPHANES: ...the dance of chance?

SHAKESPEARE: Serendipity, a word which I wish I had invented.

SOCRATES: I am now fully ready for that serendipitous dance of chance. Bring it on!!

We hear a steady sound of "white" noise in the background and then a lofty flute arching upwards.

ERIK SATIE: Only you, T.S., are aware that our little cocktail party has a drawing which will happen before we all go our separate ways.

SALVADOR DALI: Drawing? Anyone can draw anything on those blank canvases I have already signed.

ERIK SATIE: Thank you Salvador, but not that kind of drawing. We all put our names in this white hat and Eliot will choose one for the Grand Prize.

Harpo returns and silently offers to give away his white harp, even though it is not a silent auction.

ERIK SATIE: Thanks Harpo but we want you to do the drawing. Just stick your hand in there and grab one.

Harpo mimics great excitement and points animatedly to Emilia de Chatelet as the possible prize to be won with the drawing. Dickens, also just back chips in his comment.

CHARLES DICKENS: Whoever wins can get a free hypnotic trance session with me at the location of their choice.

ERIK SATIE: Thank you Charles, but that is not what we had in mind! The winner will receive an actual potion, an elixir, to bring out their creative side--instantly!

OSCAR WILDE: Absinthe?!

ERIK SATIE: No Oscar, we are talking magic and not your run-of-the-mill drink to deaden the mind and not able to fulfill.

Satie looks furtively at Joe, the bartender.

JOE: Don't look at me Monsieur Satie. I have nothing to serve here capable of prolonging life, nor do I have anything for medication to mitigate strife.

T.S. ELIOT: Satie, my friend, it is we who will provide that "essential principle" as the "drawing prize." The elixir we give will not be a mere distraction nor a panacea to disguise difficulties, be they physical or otherwise.

ERIK SATIE: Yes, there is no cure all, no panacea, no specific soporific nor anodyne.

Wilde has been growing now ever more curious about this "elixir."

OSCAR WILDE: What is it then that we will win if our number is drawn?

Van Gogh pricks up his "ear" hearing the word "drawing."

VINCENT VAN GOGH: Drawing has been my nemesis my entire life. I have continually struggled to perfect the "line."

T.S. ELIOT: This is another kind of drawing, Vincent, as Satie has already explained to Dali.

VINCENT VAN GOGH: For me there is only one--the kind that I simply cannot perfect. I am still doing sketches for my "Potato-Eaters." Can you believe it?

Out of the blue, Aristophanes blurts out from his "cloud" he has now returned to.

ARISTOPHANES: As I fill up the space of the page I don't feel the time "fly." Like sketching, it is a dreamlike process putting me in direct contact with my subconscious mind.

SIGMUND FREUD: Don't ask me to try to analyze what you are attempting to symbolize.

SALVADOR DALI: You, Aristophanes, are much more surrealist than realist.

ARISTOPHANES: My mind and writing hand, work together in a way that is both primal, real and not difficult to understand.

SALVADOR DALI: I sense you are enjoying this process of the "slow-cooking" of your idea.

We hear another strong clash of thunder just outside the mansion.

ARISTOPHANES: I definitely feel the "buzz" up here in my "cloud-of-creativity." The wings are fluttering, like so many ideas sputtering, transitory energy for our forthcoming story.

More snow has fallen outside and the temperature plummets to new lows.

ERIK SATIE: My dream of dreams: a white Christmas.

Tellenmagnum is also back now in full charge of the polar bear and the other animals who have been brought to the Cocktail Party.

JOE: I am preparing an array of special drinks for our drawing!

Harpo, who is supposed to do the drawing, has now run off again in pursuit of Emilie de Chatelet.

T.S. ELIOT: Where is Harpo now? Just look for a mute with a white cane, a white wig and a harp instead of a flute.

From outside in the storm and recent snowfall, there is more banging at the front door. Eliot hurries over to the entryway and opens the door.

T.S. ELIOT: Oh my God!

A huge elephant is seen standing there just outside the door with the snow steadily falling on its back. Dali is seated atop wearing a white Russian Cossack's hat!

SALVADOR DALI: For the drawing! Something I have always wanted to draw.

The polar bear playfully heads through the door to investigate this "White Elephant!" Satie lets his monocle drop in his surprise and excitement.

ERIK SATIE: White on white on white! A triple Christmas! With a "Salvador" riding the beast.

Tellenmagnum, still wearing his white bear coat rushes outside following his polar bear friend. Eliot turns to Dali.

T.S. ELIOT: That white elephant is the wrong size to be considered for our drawing prize.

JOE: Drinks are served!

SALVADOR DALI: The King of Siam had an extra elephant he could not give away.

Dali laughs hard and throws some white cauliflower heads into the hallway as if they were snowballs.

JOE: Not sure who ordered what, but I have French 75, Sidecar, Beefeater gin martinis and a Ramos Fizz as you requested for me to prepare, Mr. Eliot.

T.S. ELIOT: There is nothing quite so stimulating as a strong dry martini cocktail, but as long as you offered, I'll take that Beefeater gin martini stirred--Shaken martinis are forsaken.

ERIK SATIE: No absinthe for Wilde and myself?

JOE: How could I have slipped up?!

ERIK SATIE: Actually, I changed my mind. It's snowing, give me a white Russian.

Dostoevsky had stopped writing furiously on the wall of Eliot's mansion hall.

FYODOR DOSTOEVSKY: I am an idiot for trying to write a novel about the ideal of "the beautiful." My idea was to place an open-hearted, kind and positive person in society, subjected to passions, desires, lusts and greed.

T.S. ELIOT: You mean, "The Idiot?"

FYODOR DOSTOEVSKY: Of course. Could its recent publication be offered as a prize in the drawing?

ARISTOPHANES: *(From the cloud)* Only an idiot would want to read that!

SOCRATES: Stick to your "flies." I can feel them swarming.

FYODOR DOSTOEVSKY: Beauty is mysterious as well as terrible. God and devil are fighting--their battlefield is the heart.

SOCRATES: Our principal weapon to defend ourselves in this battlefield is art--the thrill of each creative start.

T.S. ELIOT: That was to be our "elixir," that we are drawing for here, when this huge "white elephant" arrived.

SALVADOR DALI: That surreal beauty of the "Unexpected." More cauliflower anyone?

ERIK SATIE: If it weren't white, I would have kept it out in the night, but I relented when it got our color scheme so incredibly right.

SOCRATES: I only hope that the "elixir" drawn is an improvement on that poison, hemlock, I was given at dawn. If it were not for its last-minute dilution, I would not be here now to be present for this new "solution."

ARISTOPHANES: As long as you are alive there, I must remain here with only my writing as a way to survive.

SOCRATES: Don't tell me that your new play, "The Flies," will be our drawing prize!

ARISTOPHANES: Like Osiris and his dismembered body torn asunder, I have taken your soul parts and pieced them together without a blunder.

SOCRATES: Back to "The Flies!"

ARISTOPHANES: That is my "business" and none of yours.

SOCRATES: A "business of flies?"--I will not be the first to be immune to their outcries.

ARISTOPHANES: Flies are fast breeders especially when they take the shape of words for speed readers. They are a pest difficult to fend off and will give you no rest.

Eliot takes a long sip of his Beefeater's gin martini.

T.S. ELIOT: Enough of all this talk. On with the party and our final drawing. Who is it who will be chosen to drink this "Elixir?"

ERIK SATIE: Will it be the luck of the draw, or will that one draw his own luck?

Lewis Carroll returns from his "rabbit hole" with a real white rabbit he now holds, looking straight at Socrates.

LEWIS CARROLL: If you drink much from a bottle marked "poison" it is certain to disagree with you sooner or later as it is no potion.

Socrates forces a half laugh, while Aristophanes roars from his high cloud.

SOCRATES: Is that the white rabbit that led you down the "hole?"

LEWIS CARROLL: Fortunately and unfortunately! T. S. Eliot asked me to bring her as the prize for whoever wins the drawing.

ERIK SATIE: By the way, that prize was supposed to be a surprise.

LEWIS CARROLL: Don't worry. It still will be!

Carroll takes off the small white hat that the rabbit was wearing and gives it to Eliot, who fills it with all the numbers of the guests present.

T.S. ELIOT: Each of you who arrived from the first to the last have a number according to when you got here.

Harpo is back and reaches in to pull out the lucky winner. He gives the piece of paper to Eliot who then reads off the number.

T.S. ELIOT: *Thirty-three! Who has that number?*

TELLENMAGNUM: It's me--I am thirty-three...thousand years old. Halfway between being and non-being. I am here and also still there.

T.S. ELIOT: As for your prize, well, you already know.

Eliot glances over at the white rabbit. Then the polar bear bounds over to where Tellenmagnum is standing, as if to guard him. The Bear then ambles on over to that "hole" as if it were in ice and there for fishing.

T.S. ELIOT: This is just the tip of that proverbial iceberg.

Satie then hands Tellenmagnum a blank white canvas which he proceeds to unroll. As this scroll unrolls it leads directly towards the outside of that "hole."

T.S. ELIOT: Where has Einstein run off to?

ALBERT EINSTEIN: I am here...and there--but mostly--there. *(He smiles.)*

T.S. ELIOT: Could you tell us about parallel universes?

ALBERT EINSTEIN: Nothing much to say; they both are and are not in play.

ARISTOPHANES: I am that "parallel" and have a lot to say, which I am furiously putting down in my new play.

ALBERT EINSTEIN: That is purely your business!

ARISTOPHANES: And the "Flies!"

We shift our attention back over to the bar area to where Hemingway is still posted, like a vigilant sentry.

ERNEST HEMINGWAY: These mojitos are not helping any more. But, contrary to what was said about me, I now have a subject to write about. This party is crazier than any of those put on by my "Lost Generation." I have suddenly found a weird kind of regeneration.

Henry Miller glides over to the bar and looks straight at Joe.

HENRY MILLER: More water! I want to get higher--into the flow.

JOE: Whoever cannot get what is going on here is welcome at my bar for some opiate infused Laudanum.

LEWIS CARROLL: I can attest that it does help to give my mind a much-needed rest. It goes well with my occasional glass of sherry.

Miller downs his glass of water gleefully and then points to Tellenmagnum.

HENRY MILLER: Looks like we have a winner here.

TELLENMAGNUM: I have won nothing which I don't already possess.

FYODOR DOSTOEVSKY: I am the one "possessed!"

He had returned to his wall to continue his mad rush of writing.

ERIK SATIE: Maybe all this is just a white lie. What am I to believe anymore T.S.?

164

T.S. ELIOT: It is in your own power to create your own fate now if it isn't too late.

JOE: I have been saving my "great juice" for the right moment. It is my own "liquid gold of old." I have been doing this awhile.

The storm outside now picks up its tempo as more lightning strikes.

JOE: Where is that "skull cup" you got from Lord Byron?

SOCRATES: I do remember that "skull cup" was then given to me almost full up.

JOE: "Doctored" by me though I don't have the Hippocrates degree.

Eliot dramatically holds up the "skull cup."

T.S. ELIOT: Fill it full of "water" you take from that "mind lake."

Tellenmagnum takes the "skull cup" and rushes outside to fill it with rain.

JOE: Aromatic, sweet-flavored, or medicated, drink its content to become elated.

HENRY MILLER: Rainwater—"water"--that's the Ultimate Elixir!

ARISTOPHANES: The storm has been hitting you over the head with that message all through our Cocktail Party. Everyone has to go through it in order to feel it.

T.S. ELIOT: To fill this "skull cup/cap" is purely symbolic. Water is inside us, inside our cells, in the cytoplasm particularly, right Charles?

CHARLES DARWIN: It is highly structured, not solid but not quite liquid either.

HERACLITUS: A river is pristine and clear only when it is flowing. The only difference is our river is vertical, not horizontal--a walking stream, the stream of the consciousness of the steamy dream.

Rilke now is back.

RAINER MARIA RILKE: Works of art are indeed always products gone to the very end of an experience where no man can go further.

ERIK SATIE: We are there now Rainier. Please Mr. Eliot, fill the skull so we may all drink.

Eliot looks down at the human skull cap and sees it is miraculously already full and ready to tap. He gasps.

T.S. ELIOT: It has filled itself!

JOE: *(Laughing and joking)* Some drinks come pre-made.

SOCRATES: It should be I who now serves the "Elixir." I, who barely survived the false one that tried to poison me.

Socrates takes the full skull cup.

166

ARISTOPHANES: From my perspective here in the cloud, that skull cap as cup now looks like a future uterus, that reproductive center of the new "word" for all of us.

SOCRATES: I see the larynx becoming this new uterus, the swirling force now has its source.

T.S. ELIOT: Then is the world no longer bound in secret knots?

ERIK SATIE: Just that ring known as the throat--our ultimate communication boat that with its own water will be able to float.

Poe now reappears with his cat, Catterina, still holding her.

EDGAR ALLAN POE: Well, I guess we do have something to remark on at the "Bear's Claw" tonight.

Ben Franklin passes by the polar bear and looks over at Balzac.

BEN FRANKLIN: Will you accompany me to the "Bear's Claw" later on?

ALBERT EINSTEIN: When you laugh you feel that spacetime dimension.

He laughs.

VINCENT VAN GOGH: I feel I can now hear with a new ear.

BEN FRANKLIN: This "Elixir" is Electric!

~ FIN ~

About the Author and Artist

David L. Laing is a visionary self-taught artist and writer currently living and working in Seattle, Washington. His works in oil, acrylic, watercolor, and pen and ink drawing have been exhibited in South America, the United States, and Europe.

In his early twenties David trekked to South America with no money, in hopes of finding or founding a "New Paris for artists." Two months later and thirty pounds lighter, he limped into São Paulo, Brazil, having traversed the entire continent overland, nearly ten thousand miles, surviving purely on his own wits and with the aid of a few helpful souls. David spent over fifteen years in Brazil writing, drawing and painting, and composing music.

Since his return to the USA, David has focused on book publishing of his own novels, art books, and compilations of his articles. *Solar Codex: A Light Odyssey* and *Notes from the Milky Way* are the first two volumes in the series of Cosmic Adventure novels. At present, he is working on three other novels to complete the series and is preparing for publication many new books of drawings, articles, dialogs, plays, and screenplays. Nearly all of David's written work is lavishly illustrated with literally hundreds of drawings, all hand-inked by him.

Connect with David L. Laing

Purchase artwork

Illustrations in this book may be purchased at ArtPal. Many more drawings and paintings from David L. Laing's other books and themed collections are available at ArtPal.com/davidllaing as fine art prints, canvas prints, custom framed prints, and even on mugs.

Connect Online

- **Website:** Find David's books, artwork and more at www.davidllaing.com

- **Email newsletter:** Subscribe at davidllaing.com for news about book releases, art collections, exhibits, and more.

- **Instagram**: Follow David at instagram.com/davidl.laing

- **Twitter:** Follow David at twitter.com/davidllaing9

- **YouTube:** See book trailers and animated illustrations at https://www.youtube.com/@davidllaing.

Artsana Video

Watch the video of David's art book, *Artsana, 35 Sacred Yoga Asanas Expressed Through Art*, at tinyurl.com/artsana-video. Produced by One Field Media, www.onefieldmedia.com, and

David L. Laing, this short film features eight extraordinary yogis, accompanied with music by Andre Feriante,
www.andreferiante.com

Books by David L. Laing

Art and Coloring Books

Higher Glyphs

Artsana: 35 Sacred Yoga Asanas Expressed Through Art

Alpha 2 Zulu: Military Alphabet Coloring Book

AlphaBetter: Coloring Book of Letters and Numbers

Ancient Runes: For Coloring and Meditation

Kolor Khmer: A Creative Cambodian Alphabet Coloring Book

Willing Evolution

Dance of the Dance

Beyond the Box—Illustrated Articles

Beyond the Box, Volume 1

Beyond the Box, Volume 2

Beyond the Box, Volume 3 [Forthcoming]

Beyond the Box, Volume 4 [Forthcoming]

Becoming Human Series—Aphorisms

Not Yet Human

Almost Human

Just Human

Fully Human

Beyond Human [Forthcoming]

Cosmic Adventure Quartet—Novels

Solar Codex: A Light Odyssey

Notes from the Milky Way

Pentagram Rising [Forthcoming]

Prometheus Reforged [Forthcoming]

Platonic Dialogue Style Books

Minds Beyond Time: A Cosmic Colloquium

Presidents in Paradise [Forthcoming]